JUNGLE DOCTOR'S
Case Book

D1824497

19

JUNGLE DOCTOR'S
Case Book

Paul White

CF4·K

10 9 8 7 6 5 4 3 2 1

Jungle Doctor's Case Book ISBN 978-1-84550-502-8

© Copyright 1952 Paul White

First published 1952

Reprinted 1953, 1954, 1956, 1958, 1961, 1963, 1967, 1970

Paperback edition 1975, Revised edition 1991

Published in 2010 by Christian Focus Publications, Geanies House, Fearn, Tain, Ross-shire, IV20 1TW, Scotland, U.K.

Fact files: © Copyright Christian Focus Publications

Paul White Productions,

4/1-5 Busaco Road, Marsfield, NSW 2122, Australia

Cover design: Daniel van Straaten

Cover illustration: Craig Howarth

Interior illustrations: Graham Wade

Printed and bound in Denmark by Norhaven A/S

Since the Jungle Doctor books were first published there have been a number of Jungle Doctors working in Mvumi Hospital, Tanzania, East Africa - some Australian, some British, a West Indian and a number of East African Jungle Doctors to name but a few.

All rights reserved. No part of this publication may be reproduced, stored in a retrieval system, or transmitted, in any form, by any means, electronic, mechanical, photocopying, recording or otherwise without the prior permission of the publisher or a licence permitting restricted copying. In the U.K. such licences are issued by the Copyright Licensing Agency, Saffron House, 6-10 Kirby Street, London, EC1 8TS. www.cla.co.uk

Scripture quotations taken from the HOLY BIBLE, NEW INTERNATIONAL VERSION. Copyright © 1973, 1978, 1984 by International Bible Society. Used by permission of Hodder & Stoughton Publishers.

Some Scripture quotations are based on the King James Version of the Bible.

African words are used throughout the book, but explained at least once within the text. A glossary is also included at the front of the book along with a key character index.

CONTENTS

Fact File: Paul White

Born in 1910 in Bowral, New South Wales, Australia, Paul had Africa in his blood for as long as he could remember. His father captured his imagination with stories of his experiences in the Boer War which left an indelible impression. His father died of meningitis in army camp in 1915, and he was left an only child without his father at five years of age. He inherited his father's storytelling gift along with a mischievous sense of humour.

He committed his life to Christ as a sixteen-year-old schoolboy and studied medicine as the next step towards missionary work in Africa. Paul and his wife, Mary, left Sydney, with their small son, David, for Tanganyika in 1938. He always thought of this as his life's work but Mary's severe illness forced their early return to Sydney in 1941. Their daughter, Rosemary, was born while they were overseas.

Within weeks of landing in Sydney Paul was invited to begin a weekly radio broadcast which spread throughout Australia as the Jungle Doctor Broadcasts - the last of these was aired in 1985. The weekly scripts for these programmes became the raw material for the Jungle Doctor hospital stories - a series of twenty books.

Paul always said he preferred life to be a 'mixed grill' and so it was: writing, working as a rheumatologist, public speaking, involvement with many Christian organisations, adapting the fable stories into multiple forms (comic books, audio cassettes, filmstrips), radio and television, and sharing his love of birds with others by producing bird song cassettes - and much more.

The books in part or whole have been translated into 109 languages.

Paul saw that although his plan to work in Africa for life was turned on its head, in God's better planning he was able to reach more people by coming home than by staying. It was a great joy to meet people over the years who told him they were on their way overseas to work in mission because of the books.

Paul's wife, Mary, died after a long illness in 1970. He married Ruth and they had the joy of working together on many new projects. He died in 1992 but the stories and fables continue to attract an enthusiastic readership of all ages.

Fact File: Tanzania

The Jungle Doctor books are based on Paul White's missionary experiences in Tanzania. Today many countries in Africa have gained their independence. This has resulted in a series of name changes. Tanganyika is one such country that has now changed its name to Tanzania.

The name Tanganyika is no longer used formally for the territory. Instead the name Tanganyika is used almost exclusively to mean the lake.

During World War I, what was then Tanganyika came under British military rule. On 9 December, 1961 it became independent. In 1964, it joined with the island of Zanzibar to form the United Republic of Tanganyika and Zanzibar, changed later in the year to the United Republic of Tanzania.

It is not only its name that has changed, this area of Africa has gone through many changes since the Jungle Doctor books were first written. Africa itself has changed. Many of the same diseases raise their heads, but treatments have advanced. However new diseases come to take their place and the work goes on.

Missions throughout Africa are often now run by African Christians and not solely by foreign nationals. There are still the same problems to overcome however. The message of the gospel thankfully never changes and brings hope to those who listen and obey. *The Jungle Doctor* books are about this work to bring health and wellbeing to Africa as well as the good news of Jesus Christ and salvation.

Fact File: Meningitis

Meningitis is inflammation of the protective membranes covering the brain and spinal cord. It may develop most prominently in response to bacteria and viruses, but also physical injury, cancer or certain drugs. It is a serious condition. The most common form is treated with antibiotics and requires close observation. A severe headache is the most common symptom followed by neck stiffness.

Fact File: Tetanus

Tetanus is a serious bacterial infection that usually results from a contaminated wound and may be fatal if not treated. The incubation period varies from a few days to a few weeks. Then there's general tiredness or weakness followed by spasm of the jaw muscles (called lockjaw). Spasms may occur spontaneously or be triggered by stimulation, such as noise or light. Other symptoms include: problems with swallowing or breathing, arching of the back and neck. The wound may go unnoticed and the infection may not seem severe, but the bacteria release a poison called a neurotoxin that attacks the nervous system and causes problems such as muscle spasm.

Anyone who has a contaminated wound may develop tetanus. Treatment should be in hospital. Depending on the severity of the case, sedation, muscle-relaxant drugs and even artificial ventilation to help breathing may be needed. With treatment, most people recover completely.

Fact File:Malaria

In Africa, a child dies from malaria every thirty seconds. Malaria is an infectious disease that kills between one and three million people every year. Most of these deaths occur with young children in Sub-Saharan Africa.

When a mosquito bites, a small amount of blood is taken which contains microscopic malaria parasites. These grow and mature in the mosquito's gut for a week or more, then travel to the salivary glands. When the mosquito next takes a blood meal, these parasites mix with the saliva and are injected into the bite.

The parasites grow and multiply in the liver and it can take as little as eight days or as long as several months before the parasites enter the red blood cells. After they mature, the infected red blood cells rupture, freeing the parasites to attack other red blood cells. Toxins released when the red cells burst cause the typical fever, chills, and flu-like malaria symptoms.

Malaria can be reduced by preventing mosquito bites with mosquito nets and insect repellents. Spraying insecticides inside houses and draining standing water where mosquitoes lay their eggs are two ways of controlling the disease.

No vaccine is currently available; preventative drugs must be taken continuously to reduce the risk of infection but these are often too expensive for people living in the third world. Malaria infections are treated through the use of drugs, such as quinine. However, drug resistance is increasingly common.

Fact File: Typhoid Fever

Typhoid is an illness caused by a particular bacteria that is transmitted by the ingestion of food or water contaminated with faeces from an infected person. The bacteria of the infected person are absorbed into the digestive tract and eliminated with the waste. Typhoid fever is characterised by a sustained fever as high as 40°C (104°F), profuse sweating, gastroenteritis, and diarrhoea. Less commonly a rash may appear.

As the disease progresses the patient often suffers from delirium and a rattling sound is heard in the lungs. Diarrhoea can occur at this stage. However, constipation is also frequent. The spleen and liver are enlarged and tender. Later on the patient may suffer from intestinal bleeding; intestinal perforation; inflammation of the brain and other organs as well as abscesses. By the end of the third week the fever abates and this continues into the fourth week.

Typhoid fever in most cases is not fatal. Antibiotics have been commonly used to treat it in developed countries. Prompt treatment reduces the case-fatality rate to approximately one per cent. When untreated, typhoid fever persists for three weeks to a month. Death occurs in between 10 per cent and 30 per cent of untreated cases.

Sanitation and hygiene are the critical measures that can be taken to prevent typhoid. Typhoid can only spread in environments where human faeces or urine are able to come into contact with food or drinking water. Careful food preparation and washing of hands are therefore crucial to preventing typhoid.

Fact File: Cholera

Cholera is an illness caused by a germ invading the bowels. The disease is usually spread by contaminated water supplies. The main symptom is watery diarrhoea which leads to fluid depletion and death from dehydration.

Most people get symptoms after two to five days. If you have cholera, you may have symptoms including: watery faeces with bits of mucus, faeces with a mild fishy smell, vomiting, tummy cramps, dehydration, fever, but this is rare and usually only in children.

The main treatment for cholera is to drink plenty of fluids to replace those lost. Antibiotics may be given to treat cholera. Antibiotics kill the bacteria which are causing the symptoms. They will also help to control diarrhoea and stop loss of fluids.

Fact File: Measles

Measles is a highly infectious viral illness. The illness causes a range of symptoms including fever, coughing and distinctive red-brown spots.

The infection is spread through the air through droplets of saliva. You can catch measles through direct contact with an infected person, or through the air when they cough or sneeze. The droplets can also survive and remain contagious on surfaces for a few hours.

Measles is most common among children who are between 1-4 years of age. The condition is most infectious after the first symptoms have appeared and before the rash has developed. Treatment for measles is normally not necessary because the body's immune system (defence against viruses) can usually fight off infection in a couple of weeks. Typically, once somebody has fought off the measles infection, they develop immunity to it.

Fact File: Pneumonia

Pneumonia is inflammation of the tissues in one or both of your lungs. It's usually caused by an infection. At the end of the airways in your lungs there are clusters of tiny air sacs called alveoli.

If you have pneumonia, these tiny sacs become inflamed and fill up with fluid. As well as making you cough, the inflammation makes it harder for you to breathe. It also means your body is less able to absorb oxygen.

Pneumonia can affect people of any age. However, in some groups of people it's more common and can be more serious. For example:

- babies, young children and elderly people,
- people who smoke, and
- people with other health conditions, such as a lung condition or a lowered immune system.

People in these groups are also more likely to need treatment in hospital. Some forms of pneumonia can be more severe than others, depending on the cause. Mild pneumonia can usually be treated at home. People who are otherwise healthy usually recover well. However, complications can develop. For people with other health conditions, pneumonia can be severe and may need to be treated in hospital. Sometimes pneumonia can be fatal. It is possible to treat it with antibiotics such as penicillin.

Fact File: Words

WORDS TO ADD EXPRESSION AND EMPHASIS: Eeeh, Eeeeeh, Eheh, Heh, Heeeh, Heya, Hoh, Kah, Koh, Jambo, Oheeh, Ugh, Yah, Yahm, Yeh, Yoh.

TANZANIAN LANGUAGES: Swahili (main language), Chigogo or Gogo (one of the 150 tribal languages)

SENTENCES/PHRASES:

Asante muno muno - Thank you very much

Baba mwana ayu yatamigwe ci - Daddy what's wrong with that child?

Chibite - Let us go

Hamba hadodo - Not even a little

Hodi? - May I come in?

Miti miswanu - The pain is gone

Sinosuma kusoma hamba kuhilika hamba cinji, nili bwete - I can't read and I can't hear. I'm worthless.'

Tanganeza puncture ya Bwana sasa hivi - Fix up the Bwana's puncture

Yali yehwanile mechila lya mbwa - This place where you make medicines is like the tail of a dog (the rainbow).

WORDS IN ALPHABETICAL ORDER

Alhamisi - Thursday	Fundi - Expert
Hongo - Behold	Ipu - Abscess
Kabisa - Completely	Kalama - Pencil
Kali sana - Very fierce	Kamweni - Good day
Kanzu - Long-flowing garment	Karani - Clerk
Karibu - Come in/welcome	Kaya - House
Knobkerrie - Knobbed stick	Kumbe - Behold!

Kwaheri - Goodbye

Mabuli-buli - Mists/cataracts

Mbisi/Mabisi - Hyena/Hyenas

Mbukweni - Good evening

Mhungo - Malaria

Mponyi - The healer

Muganga - Witchdoctor

Mwangaluka - Good day

Ndio - Yes

Nhembo - Elephant

Nzogolo - First cock crow

Shaitan - The devil

Swanu - Good

Wadala - Old women

Wugali - Porridge

Lunji - Perhaps

Mapepo - Evil spirits

Mbukwa - Good morning

Mbula - Frog

Mpiligazi - Hard worker

Mudimi - Shepherd

Mushenzi - A heathen

Mzee - Old man

N'go - No

Nje - Scorpion

Pima - Examine

Sumu - Poison

Ukutanga - Do you understand?

Wuchawi - Witchcraft

Wujimbi - Beer

Fact File: Characters

Bibi - Grandmother, a term of respect

Bwana - Dr White, main character/narrator

Daudi - Medical Assistant

George - Garage proprietor

Kefa - Hospital staff

Marita - Sister of child with burns

Matayo - Teacher

Mhutila - Water carrier

Mvula - Wife of Mwaluko

Mwenda - Staff nurse

N'gombe - Medicine man

Pepetua -Sister of child with burns

Sechelela - Senior nurse

Tumbo   Mason

Mboga - Hospital staff

Mtoto - Patient

Mwaluko - Chief from Nghati

Ngoma - Witchdoctor

Nhete - Father of child with burns

Samson - Handyman

Suliman - The Indian

Yakobo - Senior nurse

1
Arrive

The East African night was pitch dark except for a pool of light moving down the path towards my ramshackle tin-roofed house.

Daudi, my hospital assistant, put down his hurricane lantern outside the mosquito-proof door. '*Hodi*?' he called, 'May I come in?'

'*Karibu*,' I replied with one of the few Swahili words I knew. 'Welcome. Come in.'

Daudi did so and put his lamp on the table, newly-made from packing case timber.

'Daudi, am I glad to see you! I'm in trouble. I have been in your country only a matter of days. Look, I have a notebook to write down words if you will teach me.'

'I will gladly help, Bwana. Our language is not difficult. If you wish to help the women and the children of our tribe you must speak as we do. The part of Tanzania where we are living is the Ugogo country – Gogoland. The people of the tribe are the Wagogo ...'

I broke in, 'And I suppose the language is Gogo language!'

'Right!' laughed Daudi. 'Chigogo we call it. It is not a thing of difficulty. Let us start with the words for doctors. There are two sorts: *muganga* – the medicine man who cooks roots and leaves and bark and berries. We call his medicine *miti*.'

I turned up the wick of the lantern. 'Daudi, have I not heard that *miti* means trees?'

'*Eheh*, *muganga* makes his medicines from trees – different parts of them. But there is also *muchawi*. He is not a good person. His work is witchcraft. He uses charms and spells, the powered bones of poisonous snakes and the dried intestines of crocodiles. He makes *miti mititu*, black magic.' He shuddered. 'He deals with fear and demands goats and cattle for his work.' Daudi raised his eyebrows. 'Do you understand? *Ukutanga?*'

Into my notebook went *ukutanga* – to understand.

A shout came from some distance up the path and in a moment a gasping voice called, '*Hodi*.'

It was a young man, his face twisted with pain. He poured out a torrent of words, heavy with anguish. He stretched out a large foot and pointed towards his big toe.

'*Koh*,' explained Daudi. 'His name is Mboga. He works at the hospital. He is bitten and says he has severe pain.'

'What bit him?'

'*Nje!*' Again a torrent of words.

'Bwana, he says he was bitten by *nje*, the scorpion.'

I filled a syringe with local anaesthetic.

'Sit,' ordered Daudi, and held up the damaged foot. I swabbed the damaged toe and injected.

Mboga let out a deep sigh and breathed, *'Miti miswanu.'*

Daudi smiled at me. 'Good medicine. He says his pain is gone.'

Mboga blew gently on his foot. Daudi grinned. *'Mboga* means spinach or vegetable.'

Our patient stood up and wiggled his toes. He shook my hand vigorously and said slowly in English, 'Thank you very much, doctor.' Then in Chigogo, *'Asante muno muno.'* We all laughed.

Daudi picked up the hurricane lantern. 'You will soon speak our language, Bwana doctor. There is another important lesson for you to learn tonight. Here is a gift which could save your life. Never travel that path in darkness without a lantern in one hand and a knobkerrie in the other.'

He handed me a stick as long as my arm with a lump on the end of it the size of a tennis ball. 'You may travel that path a hundred times and not need it but then, *lunji,* perhaps …'

'Come, let's walk together to the hospital and perhaps, *lunji* …'

Daudi nodded. *'Chibite,* let us go.'

We set out along the path that led to the hospital. On each side were the corn stalks of last year's harvest. Doors opened and lights came on in the maternity ward. We could hear excited voices. For a moment we paused, looking at the silhouette of two big wards.

'Wadala, the old women, rejoice at the birth of a child,' explained Daudi.

We walked on under the huge centuries-old baobab trees and then beneath umbrella-like thorn trees.

Without warning Daudi gripped my arm and jerked me to one side. He grabbed my stick and crashed the knobbed end on a vague shadow coiled in the middle of the path.

'Puff adder,' he grunted. 'Truly, lamps have special usefulness.' Twice more he thumped the ground with the knobkerrie. 'Always make sure that snakes are properly dead for there is death in their mouths. Tread on him unawares and he strikes.'

We parted at the hospital gate and I turned and walked back to where I would live for some years on the thornbush plateau at the foot of the Great Rift Wall. The stars were brilliant. Here I was five hundred kilometres south of the equator. Near the horizon was the Southern Cross – a friendly sight indeed to an Australian.

From among the corn stalks came the eerie howl of a hyena. The dead snake was no longer on the path. Hyenas will eat anything. I felt profoundly thankful for the pool of light my hurricane lantern gave and for the beautifully balanced knobbed stick that I clutched firmly in my right hand. Africa certainly had its moments.

2

Father and Son

An old man sat in the shade of the hospital baobab tree. He wore a shabby black cloth and had red mud in his hair. Nimbly his fingers and toes held and polished an arrow.

He smoothed it in a couple of places with a razor-sharp home-made axe. With a grunt of approval he fitted a barb which I could see had once been a bolt from the iron highway of the Tanzania railway system. He bound this barb in place and then dipped it into a gourd full of black gum.

Kefa whispered. 'Bwana, that's *sumu*, poison, in that gourd. It's deadly stuff.'

It was fascinating watching the old man carrying out the craft which had been practised by his tribe for centuries. To me that black concoction conjured up a string of pictures of witchdoctors, murder in the night due to poison. Witchcraft! It was always close to the surface of life in that part of East Africa.

Kefa touched me on the shoulder. 'Bwana,' he whispered, 'do you know who that old man is?'

I shook my head. 'I don't know exactly. I've seen him about the village but never actually at the hospital. Who is he?'

Kefa laughed. 'Bwana, come with me and I'll show you his son.'

'Is his son an expert with arrows?'

'Bwana, I'm not sure, but he uses other things to stab people with.'

'*Hongo*, that sounds dangerous. Is he a patient in the hospital?'

'Come and see,' Kefa smiled broadly as he led me through the gateway, past the men's ward. He stopped outside a window and pointed with his stick.

I saw a Mugogo in his late twenties. He was looking down a microscope and his fingers moved skilfully over the adjustments.

'There, Bwana,' said Kefa, 'there is the son of the poisoned arrow *fundi*, expert.'

For a moment I was speechless. It was Daudi, my head dispenser. It seemed so odd. The father, an expert in jungle craft, the son skilled in dealing with tropical disease. I had spoken to the old man in Chigogo and there was the son capable in three languages.

He looked up from the eye piece of his microscope and said in good English, 'Bwana, would you mind looking at this slide?'

For the next few minutes we discussed the diagnosis. As Daudi stained another blood slide, I said, 'I've been talking to your father.'

'*Kumbe!*' he laughed. 'Bwana, I suppose he was making arrows. Behold, is he not a *fundi* at that work? It's his way of making money.'

'*Hongo*, I'm glad you didn't follow in his footsteps.'

Daudi smiled.

'Tell me, why did you leave your tribal ways and take on the hospital job?'

'It all started when I was a small boy, Bwana. I went to a village school – a little place with a few petrol boxes for desks and forms made of hardened mud. There I learned to read. The only book we had was the New Testament so, of course, I heard about Jesus.

When I heard the Gospel I decided to go God's way and to be a member of his tribe. I did this and took his book as my guide. Behold, as I read more I understood the mistakes that people made by not living his way.'

'But your father, Daudi, does he have any interest in God?'

'No, Bwana. He says that the ways of the tribe are good enough for him. You see, he puts more trust in the charm he wears round his neck than in the quinine which I would give him for his malaria. When he shivers and sweats and aches all over he thinks it's witchcraft. I know differently. Does not the microscope make it clear to me?' Daudi shook his head. '*Heh,* Bwana, in the same way, my reading of the Bible helps me to understand about sin and what it does to my life.'

A week later, coming to the hospital I found Daudi's father standing under the same baobab tree. This time he had no arrows or poison to put on them.

He greeted me in a strange husky voice. '*Heh*, Bwana, I am in great trouble, trouble which I fear will cause me to walk the path to my ancestors. Behold, I cannot eat. I can barely talk. Today I cannot swallow water. Truly, I will die.'

'Perhaps I have medicine which will help you.'

'*Lunji*, perhaps.'

I took him with me into the outpatients' room and put on a head mirror. I coaxed him into opening his mouth wide. The mirror caught the brightness of the early morning sun and reflected light down his throat. He had a large abscess behind his tonsils.

Daudi came to the door. 'Behold, Bwana doctor, my father has no joy in his throat.'

'Truly, Daudi, but we can deal with it. Is it not a large *ipu*, an abscess?'

'*Kumbe,*' croaked the old man. 'It is more than that. There are those that wish me evil. Someone has cast a spell.'

'My father,' said Daudi, 'have you not given a chicken to *muganga*, the witchdoctor? Has he not given you medicine and yet the *ipu* grows larger?'

'*Heh, heh*,' nodded the *mzee*, the old man, clutching at his throat.

My friend spoke quietly. 'It would not be wisdom to let the Bwana use his medicine.'

'Since I am going to die what harm can it do me?'

Daudi's eyes twinkled.

In English I suggested, 'For such cases as these I have some special anaesthetic. Inject this into a vein and the patient is asleep in a matter of seconds. It's excellent stuff. The surgeon has at least five minutes to do the small operation.'

Everything was prepared, all within full view of the old man. I gave the injection into his vein. For a moment I talked to him.

'Bwana, the ways of the Europeans are strange. Behold, I do not think they … are …' His voice faded away. He was unconscious. It is a quick-acting drug.

In our jungle operating theatre Daudi and I worked fast. A few moments and the abscess was no more. Everything was put away by the time Mzee opened his eyes again.

'Behold, I can speak,' he said. '*Kah*, I have thirst.'

Daudi gave him a drink. He looked across at me. 'Bwana, that's medicine. There was never anything like it in the country of Ugogo.' I said nothing. 'My *ipu* has gone.' Then in a strange voice, 'Behold, this is witchcraft.'

'Great one, this is not witchcraft but wisdom,' said Daudi. 'Behold, pain disappears in this hospital when you follow the Bwana's words. In the same way sin is blotted out when you follow the words and ways of Jesus.'

'Behold, I am too old to understand these things. I must follow the ways of the tribe as I have always done.'

To my knowledge on no occasion did he ever change his point of view.

One day I discussed it with Daudi.

'It's hard to make my father understand, Bwana.'

As I looked at father and son I thought of the tremendous changes that were coming to Africa. The old man trusted in a charm for his health and his future, and in a poisoned arrow and a primitive hoe for his food. His son had a strong faith in a living God.

3

Mpunguzi

The moon was huge. It rose deep yellow behind a grove of baobab trees that sheltered the village called Mahadze, the place of flies.

Coming towards us were a group of tribesmen wearing black cloths round their middles, coloured beads round their necks and huge ornaments in their ears. Each man carried under one arm a gourd shaped like a stool which would hold some fifty litres. Under the other arm was a scooped-out piece of wood two metres long. It was an instrument of eight strings. In their hands were clusters of little iron bells the size of an almond nut.

'*Kah*,' said Daudi, 'we've met these before, Bwana. Are they not musical instruments of the days of the grandfathers?'

The musicians greeted us and squatted down on the roots of a baobab tree. Their leader lit a hurricane lantern. They tuned their instruments and started to sing.

Daudi leant across. 'Bwana, this is good. Soon others will come. Truly they have music that is food for the ears and there will be the opportunity to talk with them.'

He was right. The musicians started with considerable gusto. People came out of the shadows.

'When they grow a little tired I will tell them the story of the village that is called Mpunguzi. This is the way that we in East Africa bring the message. Listen to them. Feel their muscles move and yours will move even as they do. Itchiness will come to your feet and you will move in rhythm. Your shoulders will also take up the beat. *Yoh*, behold, are they not *fundis!*'

They certainly produced rhythm.

There was a lull in the music. 'Bwana,' said their leader, 'we of this tribe, we Wagogo, are a proud people. We're proud of our tribe, our music and the stories we tell. Listen, let us sing you a song of the old ways, a song that our people have sung for hundreds of years, a song of sadness and of famine.'

He sat astride the large gourd. As they sang I touched Daudi's arm and whispered, 'Will you talk to them when they have finished this song?'

'*Eheh*,' He nodded. 'I have a story which is food for the ears.'

A cloud covered the moon. They finished their song and Daudi stood up. '*Hongo*, singing has much praise. As I listened I thought of the story my grandfather told me when we sat round the camp fire as children. He told of the village called Mpunguzi.

'In the days of long ago when there was much fighting between the tribes there was this village. They had many cattle and much corn. There were rumours that the tribe of the Wahehe were sending out raiding parties to fight. The men of Mpunguzi thought only of their cattle and their corn. The women cooked *ugali*. Children were born. There was not an empty stomach in the whole of the country. Day followed day and the rains were good.

'Then came a warning from the chief of the village beyond the river. "Have a care. The enemy may well come. The Wahehe have empty stomachs and could choose to come in our direction. There have been many raids."

'But day followed day and there was no sign of hostility. Then people started joking about it. Their fears became smaller. There were rumours but people only laughed and their eyes were open only for their cattle and their corn.

'One day a man came running to the village shouting, "The Wahehe are coming!"

'But the men of the village took no notice. They saw people moving in the distance along the road and they said, "It is but the people from Mchila on their way to a dance."

'They heard that there were many people coming along this road but they said, "It is only the people from Manhambulu going to a wedding."

'The women pounded the grain and prepared much porridge. The men dug in their gardens and rested in the heat of the day. But those that travelled the road were not dancers. They were not people going to a wedding. They were the enemy. In their hands were spears. To their sides were strapped sharp knives. In their minds were thoughts of war and slaughter.

'In the heat of the day when people rest the Wahehe attacked with spear and knife. There was no fighting for the people of Mpunguzi. They were not prepared. They died – men, women and children. Their cattle and their corn were taken and all that remained of the village was a smouldering ruin.'

The moon came from behind the big cloud. Daudi stood up. 'And so it is when people these days speak of those who take no notice of warnings, of those that just sit and smile when danger threatens, they say the word *Mpunguzi* and those who hear know that there is danger.'

Daudi paused. 'And we come to you with this one word from God. Do not have in your thinking the wisdom of the men of that village which finished in ashes. The word is: Jesus said, "I am the way. No man comes to the Father except through me." No man, no woman, no child.'

There was silence. The wind blew through the upper limbs of the buyu trees.

Slowly the music started again – an odd thoughtful rhythm …

Daudi stood up. 'We must return to the hospital. There is work to be done. Behold, do not forget that there is small wisdom in following the ways of the people of the village of Mpunguzi.'

4
Sechelela

The night wind howled past the house. A figure moved towards me down the path to the hospital and a voice called, '*Hodi*, Bwana.'

I opened the door. '*Karibu*. Welcome.'

In came Sechelela (which means Cheerfulness). She had for many years been head nurse of the hospital. She turned up the wick of the lantern and picked up a knobbed stick.

There was a smile on her wrinkled face. 'Bwana, more work for both of us. Twins I think.'

We walked up the path through a grove of baobab trees.

Suddenly she said, 'Not so fast. *Kumbe*, Bwana doctor, remember my legs are old.'

'*Hongo*, Sech. I've been reading of the days when your legs were young – the days when Dr Livingstone walked through these corn fields of what was then German East Africa. Truly there were troubles in those days much greater than ours.'

'*Eheh*, and there were no hospitals. If there had been my people would not have suffered as they did when my legs were young and strong.'

I opened the hospital gate for her. She walked in and then suddenly leapt aside with surprising agility bringing her stick down with a *whack!* on the hard baked earth of the hospital courtyard.

'What's up, Sech?'

'*Nje*, a scorpion, Bwana. He and his relations are many these days.'

She didn't stop to view her handiwork but crossed a moonlit courtyard, mounted some steps and opened a door.

Before us in the maternity ward lay a young woman.

Crouching in a corner were her old female relations. They mumbled suspiciously together.

Sechelela took them to task. 'Do you not greet the Bwana?'

One old woman spat. '*Kah*, he doesn't know our language or our ways. *Heeeh*, you bring him here to the house of the women.'

'*Mbukweni*, good evening,' I said in their own particular dialect.

'*Hoh*,' they said, 'he knows!' and then greeted me in Chigogo, '*Mbukweni*, Bwana.'

Sala, Sechelela's granddaughter, a trim young woman, helped me with the examination. I ordered treatment and went out into the day room to await developments.

Sechelela and I sat on three-legged stools that had been carved with an axe from the trunk of a large local tree. She yawned. '*Oheeh*, Bwana. *Heeeh*, babies, babies and more babies. Sixty-two this month so far and still five days to go.'

'Truly, Sech, we've brought eight hundred of them into the world this year and seven years ago the local women were reluctant to come near the hospital.'

She nodded her head slowly. 'Bwana, you must remember that I was the first woman ever to come to be helped by a white nurse.'

Through the window came the night noises – crickets and every now and then the deep note of a bull frog.

'*Yoh*,' said Sechelela, '*Mbula*, the frog, sings tonight. *Heeeh*, it reminds me of that awful night when I thought I would die.'

She went across to the window. I could see the stoop in her shoulders.

'Bwana, it was beyond those baobab trees where the dancing is going on now. I lay there dying in the house of my husband's father. My first three babies had already died. I followed the ways of the tribe and fed them on porridge and they died, Bwana. My fourth baby had been born at sunset. *Kumbe*, there was great trouble. I was bleeding to death. The old women could do nothing. I could feel death coming closer.

'Outside the people of the village danced. In my mind I can hear it still – the drums and the singing and the howling of hyenas. And then came a European, a woman. She had been in the village not many days. There were those that tried to thrust her out. She had courage and said, "I have medicines. They will help her. Let me try them." What she did I did not know then but I have done it myself hundreds of times since.

'Strong medicine was given me. I swallowed it with difficulty. She knelt beside me and held up my head and gave me hot sweet drinks and the bleeding stopped and death was cheated. I knew it as I lay there, Bwana, and heard those drums and heard the voice of *Mbula*, the frog. I shall never forget that night.'

Suddenly her tone changed. She was at the door leading into the maternity ward. 'Don't you dare to move,' she ordered, 'not one step, not even one.'

The old women shuffled back to their seats in the corner.

'*Kah*,' said Sechelela, 'they are one of our great nuisances. Those old women, the *wadala*, do dreadful things. But I was telling you … the Bibi gave me medicine that brought strength back to my body. She talked to me much about life and I told her that I had fear of death. She agreed that I was right to fear because sin means death to the soul. She explained it to me, Bwana. She told me about the baby son of God. Her words sank into me like rain after many days of drought.

'Then I heard how Jesus grew and lived and taught and healed and died, how they nailed him to a cross …' There was a catch in her voice. 'Bwana, he died the just one for the unjust to bring us to God. So I prayed to God and asked him to give me the life that is everlasting. I realised Jesus was alive. He had risen from the dead. *Heeh*, Bwana, I said that I would live his way and obey him.

'It was not easy. But *hongo!* when my sixth child was born, the mother of Sala here, she was born in the little room that Bibi had built – the place where she gave medicine to those who would come. Many told me "Your child will die," and I answered, "*Kumbe*, they all have so far," but this time, Bwana, it was different. Hefsi lived and … '

'Bwana,' came Sala's voice, 'come. Mama Seche, come.'

I worked extremely hard for the next half hour. When Sechelela undid the tapes of my mask and the buttons of my gown I felt that those two dusky pink African babies had an excellent chance of living to be as old as Sechelela if only the old women of the tribe could be kept from their usual tricks.

The young mother was speaking. I bent down. 'Bwana, truly your being here is the goodness of God. I could have suffered for days unless you had helped.'

'Truly,' agreed Sechelela, 'but the Bwana and the nurses knew exactly what to do.'

Again I went into the day room and made an entry in the record book. 'Sixty-three babies this month, Sech.'

'No, Bwana, sixty-four. These last two were twins.' She smiled at me. '*Eeeh*, three lives saved before midnight. Not a bad evening's work, *eh*, Bwana?'

Not so long ago Sechelela died. She was very old and very highly respected – a wonderful person. CMS hospitals have many like her who give their lives for God and the welfare of others.

5
Handful of Seed

Daudi laughed. 'They called him Samson, Bwana, because he was tall and strong and a man of considerable usefulness.'

'He's the man I need for a difficult job. Would you ask him to write to the chief of the village called Nhundulu?'

A few minutes later Samson stood in the doorway. '*Hodi,* Bwana. Daudi tells me you have a work of difficulty for me to do.'

'It's that chief who lives beyond the rocks where we saw three giraffe on our last safari.'

'It is not an easy thing you ask, Bwana. He is a man of trouble.'

'You will need all your wisdom, Samson, but these days many women from his village do not come to the hospital. Their children are sick, many of them die. I would speak with the chief and the women of his village. Behold, we have medicines which will help them and I would like to show them what we can do at the hospital.'

Samson shook his head. 'That village is a place where the witchdoctor speaks with strength and he has powerful *wuchawi*, witchcraft.'

Daudi looked up from his microscope. 'But there was a time when the chief of that village had bad toothache and did not the Bwana help him greatly with his dental forceps?'

Samson smiled. 'I'll write the letter, Bwana.'

'Good. And before you go, come away from that microscope, Daudi, and let's ask God to help us in the matter.'

We knelt round a petrol box on the floor and each prayed that God would help us to bring the Good News to the people of that jungle village.

An hour later I saw my tall African helper walk out through the hospital gate, over the dry river bed and through the millet gardens towards the pile of granite boulders just visible on the horizon. I had reason to believe that seven out of every ten children in that part of the country died before they had their first birthday.

Two days later a messenger arrived. 'The chief would have joy if the Bwana would visit his village. He will receive you on *Alhamisi*, on Thursday. A room will be made ready in his own house. He personally will see that the women come and to prove

his goodwill towards you he has sent a gourd full of eggs.' There proved to be thirty-four of them, of which twenty-two were decidedly off-colour.

We drove over a rough patch of road in the early morning and walked the final six kilometres through corn fields along one of the most fertile stretches in the country. The crops were two metres high. The pathway wound through the middle of it. Everybody seemed busy scaring away the small weaver birds which flew in by the thousand to feed on ripening seed.

Men stood ready with bows and arrows to shoot at the monkeys who scampered out of the jungle, pulled whole ears of corn and rushed back to the shelter of the trees. Old men and women sat on raised platforms and tugged long ropes stretching above the crops. Movement and clatter kept both birds and animals away from the ripening harvest.

'*Koh*,' said Sechelela, who had come with us. 'Many people will not come for medicine today. They will say, "Should we leave our crops to be eaten by the birds? Is it not better to have sickness than to die of starvation?"'

When we arrived at the village there were twenty-seven women and children waiting for us. The chief was dressed in a newly ironed *kanzu* – a long flowing nightshirt-like garment.

He greeted me. 'Bwana, you are welcome to visit our village. Behold, I have made many preparations for you. There is a place for you to *pima*, to examine, those who have sicknesses.'

I ducked my head to enter a room of his mud-and-wattle house. It was barely high enough for me to stand up. There was an overpowering smell from the floor which told of a mixture of cow manure and mud, trodden in till it was hard.

'It is a thing of wisdom to have flooring like that,' said Seche. 'Fleas don't breed in that sort of floor.'

I thought how wise they were.

The chief brought me a three-legged stool and unobtrusively brushed off a cockroach which fell from the roof. Soon we were ready to start. Sechelela had a native bed brought in for the comfort of the sick.

One woman objected. She pointed in my direction.

'Send him out. We will not tell him the secrets of our sickness.'

'*Kumbe*,' sniffed Sechelela, 'is he not the doctor? Does he not know everything?'

This was rather too much for me but I had to turn my laughter into a carefully disguised cough.

Before long, case after case was examined and medicine given. Everyone seemed to have malaria. Many showed a wide variety of tropical diseases and I heard the pathetic story of how child after child had died from meningitis, measles, typhoid and cholera. Flies swarmed everywhere and crawled unresisted into the eyes of the children and babies. Some were given injections.

Thankfully I came out of the stuffy atmosphere of the African house into the open air. I found a collection of people who had come to greet me and to 'taste' my medicine.

'Where is your pain? What are the troubles of your body?'

'*Koh*,' I was told again and again, 'we have none but we've come to taste your medicine.'

Sechelela tapped me on the shoulder and whispered, 'Bwana, you must give them medicine. There will be great disappointment if they do not get any. Behold, we have a big bottle of Epsom Salts here. Let us mix that up and give it to them. It will bring them deep satisfaction.'

And so everyone crowded into the shade of an umbrella tree and solemnly drank a strong dose of Epsom Salts. They smacked their lips and told one another, '*Yah*, truly, that was medicine!'

As they stood there listening, Sechelela told them the story that Jesus had told of the sower and the seed.

They all nodded their heads. Was not this the time when much sowing was going on?

'Behold,' she said, 'do we not know how some of the seed we plant does not come up? Behold, in other places the weeds thrive and choke the young corn. And do not the birds take much of the seed?'

'*Eheh*,' nodded the African gardeners, 'does not this happen?'

'But,' said Sechelela, 'there is the good prepared ground. Into this the seed falls and grows and there can be a big crop.'

Again the people agreed.

'*Eheh*,' said the chief. 'These are words we understand. *Koh*, Bwana, I perceive that this story is a riddle. What is the meaning behind it? Tell us, what is the meaning?'

'Behold, Great One, the story is of the person who plants the crop. It was told by Jesus, the Son of God, and just as you have asked for the meaning, so did those that followed Jesus. The words of God are the seed. Jesus said of them, "When a man hears the words about the Kingdom of God but does not understand them, then *Shaitan*, the devil, comes and takes away what has been sown in the mind of the person who listens."

'Sechelela told you what happens when the seed falls on the hard trodden path. Nothing grows there. When seed falls on stony ground, this is the man who hears the word and at the beginning is filled with happiness and enthusiasm. Then he has small wish to obey God's words. The earth is too shallow. His seed strikes no roots. When he finds the way hard, he turns his back on the ways of God.

'He who receives the seed among the weeds is the man who hears the word but all the worries of his everyday living and his desire for much money, *heeh*, this stifles the word and it does not grow.

'But the one who hears the word and receives it into his thinking and doing, he is the man who hears and understands. For such people there is a harvest.'

'*Heeeh*,' the chief sighed. 'Bwana, these are hard words.'

'Truly, Great One, read the words of God in this book.' I gave him a New Testament then I pointed to my box with all the medicines and injections in it. 'Behold, these medicines will help your body to be well. You will lose your pain and your fever. But in this book is the answer to every problem.'

'Behold,' exclaimed the chief, 'we would need a teacher to read the words to us and to teach us to understand them.'

From behind the crowd of people listening a sixteen-year-old boy came forward. 'Great One,' he ventured, 'behold, when I was in the hospital of the CMS, I

44

had *mhungo*, malaria fever. I was weak but when I grew strong I learned to read and to read God's book. Behold, I will read for you the words of the book the Bwana has given to you.'

'*Kwaheri*,' we farewelled them.

As we walked through the corn Sechelela said, 'Bwana, the boy who spoke, he is the one who heard the word. Behold, there is a harvest in his heart.'

'*Eheh*, that will be a good one, and the sowing will go on through him in this village.'

6
Dynamite

I crouched on the shady side of our battered truck on the Great North Road.

An Indian's lorry rolled by driven by an Arab. It was more than overloaded with bags of millet and maize. On top of this sat a dozen Africans, singing enthusiastically. They yelled a greeting to me. I waved back as I put a patch on a puncture. With an old pair of dental forceps I dragged out a 5-centimetre thorn from the tyre. It was one of the hold-ups that a jungle doctor learned to expect. I put the tube back, screwed in the valve and jumped on the wheel to force the cover back into position and pumped up the tyre. Then, as I let down the jack, I found that the front tyre was flat also.

Behind me I heard the rattle of a vehicle and half-a-minute later, with a grinding of brakes, a Public Works Department lorry pulled up.

'Hello, doctor,' greeted the cheery official. His Herculean task was to keep this part of the vital

East African highway in repair. 'Having a spot of trouble?'

I wiped the sweat from my brow with a dusty hand.

'Punctures, George,' I groaned. 'Punctures!'

He laughed again and turned to his assistant. *'Tanganeza puncture ya Bwana sasa hivi,'* he said in Swahili. 'Fix up the Bwana's puncture.' Then to me, 'Come and have a cuppa.'

I surrendered my tools to a smiling African and soon was telling my friend of our various adventures. 'It's this way, George. Our job is booming. The more success we have, the more patients we get. And the more patients we get, the more success we have.'

The PWD man laughed and refilled my cup. 'And so, Doctor, what are you doing about it?'

'I'm turning the old verandah into a new maternity ward and I reckon I can do the whole job for a hundred shillings. But it means quarrying stone. I've got three strong men with hammers and crowbars and wedges but they don't make much headway on quarrying the granite near Mvumi. Now give me the benefit of your expert knowledge. What's your fee?'

'I would say ten shillings,' suggested George.

'That's the cost of saving a life with us. The consultation fee at Mvumi is a cent or a bundle of sticks or a handful of grain or an egg.'

Muscular George whistled and pulled two five shilling notes from his pocket. 'I didn't realise you could do things as cheaply as that. Anyway, here's a life.' He put the notes into my hand.

Little did he realise how low our finances were. In a week I needed to pay the wages and there was not nearly enough money to cover them.

'Bwana,' reported the puncture-repairer, 'the work is finished.'

'*Asante*,' I replied.

'Well, doc,' said the PWD man, 'why not dynamite that rock? I'll come and do it for you on Saturday afternoon.'

'Great stuff,' I replied. 'Thanks so much.' I waved goodbye as he disappeared in a cloud of dust.

Later that afternoon I went to our quarry. There were three men working. All of them had had leprosy. In each case the disease was burnt out. There was no trace of infection but the ravages of the disease were painfully visible in the lack of toe joints and finger joints. Their faces were scarred by the activities of this all-too-common disease.

They greeted me. '*Yoh*, Bwana, this is work! This stone is hard and will not crack. It is time wasted. Behold, see this is all that we have to show for our work.' They pointed to a heap. It certainly was not enough to keep the masons going on our new project.

There was one big granite boulder. Pointing to it I said, 'What about that bit?'

They shook their heads. 'Bwana, it's too hard.'

I nodded. 'Do you remember in the Bible it says that Jesus is the stone which the builders rejected and behold, he became the chief stone in the whole building?'

'Truly,' agreed one of the men, 'if Jesus had not come what would life be like for such as we are? We would have nothing to look forward to in this life ...' He held up his mutilated hand, 'But, Bwana, there are so many who don't understand these things.'

'You're right. Let's preach a parable to them. Go round the villages and say that there is a stone the Bwana says he will break in two. They will be the main stones in the building of the new ward. Tell them that for days you have tried to crack it but, without success. Do that and we'll teach them a lesson they'll never forget.'

I showed them how to drill holes in this large granite boulder. One of them who was an expert blacksmith soon had a charcoal fire going. This he blew with an ingenious bellows which he contrived from fire-baked clay and a goat's skin.

On an old piece of railway track which he used as an anvil he sharpened drills and crowbars. Soon sizeable holes were drilled in the granite.

Apparently my quarrymen had done their job well for people came to look at the stone and laughed scornfully. 'Behold, no one could crack that rock. It's not possible.'

'*Yoh*' said one of the quarrymen, 'behold the hearts of many people are like that but the Bwana tells us of the God who has power to crack hearts of stone.'

'*Yoh!*' sneered one broad-shouldered man named Mugoli, the rich one, who prided himself on his disbelief. 'If the Bwana can crack that stone, perhaps I would listen to the story of the power that cracks hearts.'

There were smiles from some of his cronies.

I had come up in time to hear this. 'Be here on Saturday, Mugoli, and see it happen,' I suggested. 'We will soon have that stone in many pieces. You will hear an explosion that will make you run for your life.'

'*Eeeeh*,' Mugoli laughed, 'this is impossible.'

'*Hongo*,' I said, 'be with us on Saturday then … '

When the end of the week arrived there was a crowd to watch proceedings. George from the PWD turned up armed with dynamite, fuses and drills. He looked at the bored holes and held out the dynamite for the inspection of the crowd.

'*Yoh*,' sneered Mugoli, 'I'm not frightened of that.'

'Listen,' I warned, 'there is danger. If you do not run when the Bwana Fundi here lights that piece of string that fizzes then, behold, you may be badly hurt.'

Everybody was most impressed except Mugoli who sniffed, 'I have no fear. It can't hurt me.' He talked loudly. 'I do not worship the God of the Europeans. My ancestors are more important for me.'

'But,' said Daudi, 'Jesus Christ, God's Son, was never in Europe. As a child he lived in Egypt. He was not a European, nor yet an African, but he was the link between them.'

Mugoli sneered again. 'I do not believe in him. I do not believe in the words of his book. I will not believe anything I cannot understand.'

I held up one of the greasy packets of dynamite. 'Listen, O loud talker, can you understand this? This stuff is medicine of considerable power that will split that rock?'

But Mugoli, thoroughly pleased with the impression he was making, retorted, '*Yoh*, it could not, *hamba hadodo*, not even a little.'

George tamped down the charge, fixed the fuse and shouted, 'Run, all of you! Hide behind rocks or in holes in the ground. After I light this fuse soon there will be a loud bang and the rock will be torn by the strength of this medicine.'

There was a scurry and even Mugoli moved back a few paces. He leaned against the trunk of a large baobab tree. I moved to a safe distance and crouched behind a rock. I smiled as I saw scores of the local tribe, thoroughly scared, waiting to see what would happen.

With a yell to 'look out!' my friend touched off the fuse and ran to crouch beside me.

There was a dead silence and in it Mugoli moved forward from his vantage point. 'Behold,' he sneered, 'nothing happened. It was a lie. Who would believe the words of the Bwana? Behold, he is not one …'

At that moment the dynamite exploded with a roar. Bits of stone were showered down – one of them cruising perilously close to the doubter. With a yell that rivalled the explosion he took to his heels followed by the laughter of the assembled Africans. When they saw us approach the rock which was split neatly in pieces they gathered confidence and came round.

'There,' said the PWD expert, 'that will show you that we do not talk lies.'

Daudi, who had been quietly watching proceedings, put up his hands. 'Tomorrow I want you to come with the doubting one to the church and I will tell you the story of today.'

Next morning he preached with his Bible in one hand and a stick of dynamite in the other. It certainly was a powerful talk.

'"I am not ashamed of the Gospel – the Good News – of Jesus Christ because it is the power of God for the salvation of everyone who believes." Through this power sin is conquered and kept conquered and a way is opened up for us to have life forever as well as to have the help of God with us here on earth.'

In the back seat, sitting extremely quietly, was Mugoli with all the bounce taken out of him. He turned up at the hospital as new piles of stone were brought up and the masons completed a job that was vitally important for the expansion of our hospital work. Day after day he watched as the dynamite-split stone was built in.

One day I found him talking to one of the quarrymen.

'Behold,' said the workman, 'it says in God's book that many people will not believe in Jesus because he does not offer an easy life to those who follow him. He offers hard toil – no laziness and no easy road.' He held up his scarred hands.

'But for leprosy I would never have understood about God nor bothered to think about him.'

'I want to follow my own way,' snorted Mugoli and strode away from the hospital.

The quarryman took up his crowbar again and after prizing out a large square of granite turned to me, 'Bwana, how true are Jesus' words that the road to death and destruction is broad, easy, and kind to the feet.'

I nodded. 'Especially when it is softened by much wealth.'

7
Chief's Eye

It was one of those burning hot days when heat shimmered over the East African plains. The baobab trees stood out against the glare and it was an effort even to breathe.

It was the usual thing – more than half of the tropical night had been spent in our maternity ward and I was tired. I sweltered in my mud-brick office.

'*Hodi*,' came a voice.

'*Karibu*,' I replied.

Daudi appeared. 'Bwana, we have a visitor, Mwaluko, the chief from Nghati – a rich man with many cows.'

'*Hongo*, Daudi, I remember him. We did his cataracts last June.'

'*Heya*, Bwana, and he's back today. He wants to tell you of all that it means to him. But I warn you, Bwana, he is a man of many words.'

'Bring him in, Daudi, and I'll listen to what he has to say. I feel much more like words than works today.'

A moment later I was solemnly shaking hands with an old man. I asked about his health, his garden, his home, his cattle and his wives. Incidentally there were seven of these and thereby hangs this tale.

At long last he sat down on the three-legged stool and in a deep voice started his story.

'Behold, Bwana, I am an important chief with large herds, a big house and my seven wives. I am a chief who rides on a donkey. Before I came to the hospital, when my eyes were in trouble I was *mushenzi*, a heathen. I did not know God. Six of my wives were like me but one was not. She was called Mvula.'

'*Kumbe!* And what was she?'

'She, Bwana, was a Christian. Some time before people who had built a little church of mud-and-wicker-work in the next village believed in God. Mvula went each Sunday to hear the words that they spoke but all my other wives laughed at her. It was about this time, Bwana, that *mabuli-buli*, mists, began to appear before my eyes. I rubbed them but the mists

56

remained. Days passed. The mist grew thicker and thicker. My sight became dimmer and dimmer and I could not see. I could not see my wives or my cows or my house.

'So I said to myself, "I must go to the witchdoctor. Perhaps he may be able to give me medicine to give me back my sight." Five of my counsellors and two of my wives led me to the witchdoctor's house and helped me to climb down from my white donkey. I made a *shauri*, a bargain, with the witchdoctor. But, *hongo!* he had seen me coming a long way off and he said in his heart, "Here comes the chief. He seeks medicine. He is a rich man so I will be able to ask a big gift from him." To me he said, "I can make your eyes better but it is medicine of difficulty to cook. You will see again if you give me that big bull of yours. I will dig roots and shred bark and cook them and you will drink and in a few days light will return to your eyes.'

'"I will certainly give you the bull," I answered and I sent a messenger to Ndalu, my herdsman, telling him to send me the biggest bull immediately so that I might receive my sight again. When the bull was brought the

witchdoctor examined it carefully, went away to the jungle and came back with a basket containing leaves and roots. He put them in a big clay pot with honey and the liver of a white cock and cooked them for an hour.

'"Your medicine is ready," he said and he took the pot in which was brown slimy stuff and he made me drink it all. *Ugh!* It brought no joy to my stomach. Behold my inside turned this way and that way for days but I thought it would be worth it if I could see.'

'My wives came to help me for the pain was great. "What does it matter" I thought, "if only I can see again?" But many days passed and no light came so I knew I had been deceived by *Muganga*. He had lied to me. I was in great distress for many days.

'Then one of the old men came to me and said, "Great One, there is a medicine man who lives at the village of Ihogolo. Men say he has much wisdom. Perhaps he will help your blindness."

"*Koh*," I replied, "I will go anywhere if I can but see again. There is no joy in this darkness."

'So I mounted my donkey again and travelled many hours through lion country. Muganga, the medicine man said, "Give me that spear and the shoes that you are wearing and I will make your eyes better."'

The old chief stretched out his hands towards me. 'Behold, Bwana, I had a beautiful long, sharp, shiny spear. It had belonged to my father and was precious to me. And my shoes – I had bought them for many shillings from Hamid the Arab in the big town. But what are shoes and spears in comparison with eyesight? So I told the medicine man to work his cure. He chewed up something in his mouth and spat it in my eyes. *Eeeeh*, it burned. For days I groaned in my house. Then I realised that I had been deceived once again.

'Again my counsellors persuaded me to go to another witchdoctor. He said, "Give me the white donkey on which you ride and I will heal your eyes." So I gave him my beautiful donkey and he took some charms and hung them round my neck and round my wrists and said, "These have great power in them. Wear them and in a few days' time your sight will be restored." See … the old man handed me some pieces of cowhide. As I examined them he spat forcibly through the doorway. '*Kah*, Bwana, I was deceived for the third time. Then great was my sorrow because not only were my eyes no better but I had lost my bull and my donkey, my spear and my shoes.'

'O Chief,' I sympathised, 'great was your sorrow indeed. But why did you not come to our hospital?'

'It was this way, Bwana. One Sunday Mvula came home from church and said, "O Chief, the Christians at the church where I go to worship God tell me that at Mvumi is a hospital of the people of God. There he cures many diseases and even blind people have gone there and found their eyesight again."

'I called my counsellors together again and said, "Hear the words of my wife, Mvula. Let us go to Mvumi."

'The next day we started on the safari. A strong *mzee*, an elder, went in front holding one end of a long stick. I followed holding the other end. It was a long journey. How I longed for my strong leather shoes and for my white donkey. Thorns pierced my feet and my legs were filled with tiredness.

'At last we arrived and I rested in a comfortable bed such as I have never slept in before. Three times each day came a nurse and rubbed *mafuta*, ointment, round my eyes and poured blue medicine into them. But one day they cut my eyelashes short with scissors and said, "Tomorrow the Bwana will cut your eyes and you will be able to see."

'"*Yoh*," I muttered, "my misery is great. Will not the pain be much? My troubles are more than I can bear. I have suffered many things of many witchdoctors and still I cannot see."

'"You need not be afraid," said Mboga, "for the Bwana will put medicine into your eyes before he cuts them, medicine that will take away pain, but you must be quiet when he cuts your eye. You must remain perfectly still. You must look up or down at your feet exactly as the Bwana says. If you don't, or if you shake with fear, you will ruin his work and your eyes will have no light."

'"I will do as you say – anything – if light comes back to my eyes."

'Then, Bwana, you prayed and asked God himself to help me – and you also.

'Next day I walked to the place where you work with your little knife. They lay me on a table. They put the painkilling medicine in my eyes. My face was covered. Cold things kept my eyes open. Again they prayed. I lifted up my heart to God and asked that I might see.

'You said, "Look up." I looked up. You said, "Look down" and I looked down. You said, "Quietly, now. Gently now."

'And then I heard you sigh and my joy was great for behold there was light. I could see people moving. Then I saw your face and you said, "What was that?"

'"A finger," I replied. "And that?"

'"Three fingers." Oh, joy filled my voice! All the hospital helpers standing around laughed with happiness and you said, "No keep still. Don't get excited. Your eyes must be bandaged."

'How quietly I lay. *Yoh*, the bed was hard. My bones stuck through my skin but it was worth it all. And each day Daudi came and talked to me about God.

'When the bandages came off I said, "Now I know that only the people of God speak the truth. Three times I have been deceived by cunning men and gave of my possessions without getting better but I came here to the hospital and you gave me back my sight."

'I know these words which I have heard about God and about Jesus are true. I know, Bwana, that Jesus is my Saviour and that I have eternal life because of him.

'Behold, now I go to church with Mvula. My other wives also go. They have ceased to laugh at her for was it not through her word that I am able to see?'

My tiredness lifted and the day seemed almost comfortable.

8
Child to Child

'Bwana,' said Daudi, 'a woman has come from a village beyond the western hills. She is no stranger to the hospital. She has four children. All of them had measles and have been treated by our measles squad. Three of her children are well but she thinks this one is blind. Bwana, she has walked twenty kilometres today, setting out at *nzogolo*, first cock crow.'

From the back view I could see the baby held on her back by an ingenious contraption made from a goat skin and some strips of cloth. Holding her hand was a four-year-old girl. Flies swarmed round her eyes and she whimpered all the time.

'*Mbukwa*, good morning,' I greeted.

The woman spoke in a voice full of emotion. Her story was that this child has lost her cough and was happy until three days before when she noticed that the child could not see.

I moved over to have a look. There was a scream from the little girl who buried her face in her mother's side. She shut her eyelids so tightly that it was impossible to catch even a glimpse of the eye itself.

I spoke quietly to the mother. 'Let her understand that I like her and she will not be hurt in any way.'

The child opened her eyes a minute crack to look at me. At that moment my small son who was about the same age as the child herself came walking to me. He was dressed in a sunsuit.

Taking my hand he said, *'Baba mwana ayu yatamigwe ci*. Daddy, what's wrong with that child?'

'Kah'' exclaimed the little girl. 'He speaks our language.' Her eyes opened a little more. *'Hongo,'* she went on, 'and he's white – all of him.'

David went over to her and showed her the various animals on his sunsuit. Child gained the confidence of child and standing at a distance I saw her eyes open sufficiently for me to see two ugly ulcers, each of which, if left, would erode through the cornea and leave her blind for life.

As the children exchanged confidences I beckoned to the mother and whispered, 'Don't fear. We'll be able to help, but you will need to stay in hospital with her for perhaps seven days.'

'Hongo,' said the woman, 'there will be trouble at home. My husband will complain. These are the days when there are many birds robbing the crops and we spend much time scaring them away.'

'If you wish, leave the child with us. We will look after her.'

The woman shook her head. 'I could not do that.'

'At any rate, take the child round to the ward and we'll put her to sleep.'

'But, Bwana, the child will fight and you will not be able to do it.'

'Behold, the child will sleep and while she sleeps I will treat the ulcers.'

I went back into the theatre and took David with me. 'My son, will you do something for me?' I poured medicine from two bottles into a measuring glass.

'Yes, Daddy,' said the youngster in English. 'What do I do?'

'Take this to the little girl and ask her to drink it for you.'

Carefully I kept out of sight and watched those two four-year-olds. It was a dramatic moment. What he

said I did not hear but I saw him take the medicine to her. She dipped her finger into it. I had carefully put strong syrup with the sleeping medicine and this tickled the child's palate so much that she drank it down greedily.

David came across to me again. 'Daddy, she wants more.'

I filled the glass again, this time with pure syrup, but I brought it out myself. Lifting her scarred eyes the child whimpered, 'I don't want it from you. Let him give it to me.' I smiled and handed the medicine to my son.

'Better sit in the sun,' I suggested to the mother, 'or, if you like, in the shade of this tree and let the little one sit on your knee.'

An hour later the girl was sound asleep. The medicine worked splendidly. Gently the mother carried her into the operating room and the anaesthetic was given. Daudi stood beside me with a number of small bottles and some sharpened matchsticks.

'*Hongo*,' he said as I washed the eyes out with antiseptic solution, 'there, Bwana, is what happens to hundreds and hundreds of African children. They get measles and they are not allowed to sleep. Their eyes are open all the time. They cry until there are no more tears. They rub their eyes and the flies swarm in. Then a little ulcer starts. No one would notice it except us. And then it gets bigger and bigger until …'

'Stop there for a moment, Daudi. I'm going to fix this ulcer.'

I peered at it through a magnifying glass. 'It's a ticklish one, this. It's deep, so deep that the thickness of a piece of paper more and it would be right into the eye.'

'*Koh*,' grunted Daudi.

I took up a sharpened matchstick and prayed, 'Oh God, please direct my hand.'

I held my breath and guided the matchstick dipped in antiseptic round the edges of the ulcer.

'Drops, Daudi, please.'

I put them in and bandaged the eyes.

'You were saying, Daudi, that the ulcer gets bigger and bigger and bigger until …'

'*Heeeh*, Bwana, the ulcer eats into the eye and then comes blindness and often death.'

'And yet it starts in such a small way. Unless you know what to look for you wouldn't even notice it.'

'True, Bwana, but we do know what to look for and we do know how to treat it.'

We called the mother. She picked up her daughter and carried her off to the ward.

As we put away the various medicines and instruments I said, 'Daudi, I was thinking of something Jesus said about eyes.'

'What was that, Bwana?'

'He said, "Why do you look at the speck of sawdust in your brother's eye and take no notice of the log in your own eye?"

'Before we look for the mistakes and sins in other people, Jesus wants us to look for them in our own life.'

9

Septic Focus

Kefa had been giving trouble. He was pig-headed and stubborn and difficult. His work was slovenly. I called him into my office.

'Are you not feeling well these days, Kefa?'

'I'm all right, Bwana,' He shrugged.

'Has your wife lost her skill in cooking?'

'No, Bwana.'

'I see … it's like that! Well, listen. There was a man named Meno, the tooth. At the roots of this tooth there was a germ. That germ married, lived happily and had a very large family. Before long his tribe was a large and prosperous one – so prosperous that the man's tooth ached and ached as the germ village increased in size.

'Behold, Meno lost his interest in work. He beat his children. He thrashed his wife. Misery plagued his life till one day he came to us. We removed that tooth and destroyed the village of germs. Then, behold, the man's smile returned. He loved his wife and his children. His garden was the best in the village.'

'*Yoh*,' grunted Kefa, 'Bwana, what are you talking about?'

'You, and I'm telling you there's something wrong.'

'There's nothing wrong,' growled Kefa. 'I do not beat my wife.'

'No,' I replied, 'truly. But listen, there was a man walking along the path. Suddenly he yelled. A thorn had gone into his foot. He had hot anger but the thorn broke off because he removed it with small skill and then limped on his way. In a few days his foot swelled and became full of pain. He hobbled round with a stick. His temper became vile and his wife and children kept out of his way. He did not want his food and he did not recover till those of the hospital operated and removed the part of the thorn which remained and the abscess that surrounded it.'

'*Yoh*,' snorted Kefa. 'Bwana, what are you talking about?'

'I'm talking about you. There is something in you that is wrong and you will not recover until you get rid of it.'

'*Eeeh*,' Kefa growled and put his head in his hands. 'Bwana, if you had been angry with me it would have been all right. If you had raised your voice and said many hard things it would have pleased me but behold, you speak softy. You tell me stories that give me no joy.'

I smiled. 'Then what's the trouble, Kefa?'

'Bwana, I have preached the words of God with my mouth but my heart has been wrong. I am not strong enough. It is better for me to leave the work and return to the village, to return to witchcraft, to the making of much beer and evil living.'

I took a pencil from my pocket and attempted to balance it on the table. Each time it fell down with a clatter. After the sixth time my hospital helper looked at me irritably.

'Oh, don't do that, Bwana. It annoys me and makes my head ache.'

I smiled. 'Kefa, why doesn't the pencil stand up by itself?'

'It's not able to do so, Bwana. It's too thin. Its legs are not strong enough.'

I put my hands round the pencil and grasped it tightly.

'And now?'

'*Hongo,*' he said, 'that's different. You're holding it.'

'Does it fall?'

'It cannot fall, Bwana, because you are strong and much bigger than a mere pencil.'

I picked up a New Testament which had pride of place among my medical books.

'Listen, Kefa, God's book says, "I can do all things through Christ who strengthens me." You've been trying to do everything by yourself. You're like the pencil. You need the strong hand of God to strengthen you and help you. And don't forget that if you confess your sin to God he will forgive you. The Lord Jesus Christ paid the price when he was crucified. You repented and you're forgiven.'

He shook his head slowly and without another word being spoken, we knelt down and prayed together.

As we stood up he grasped my hand. 'Thank you, Bwana. Truly I understand.'

'Right. And Kefa, should you look like trouble again, I will call you *Kalama*, Pencil, and you and I and God will understand.'

At that moment Daudi's voice came from outside. 'Where's Bwana?'

'Here I am. What's the matter?'

'A child – he has broken his arm. Great trouble. It happened three weeks ago. There's much infection through the witchdoctor's work. *Kumbe*, it smells, that arm.'

The last statement was so true that you merely had to follow your nose to find the boy with terror written in his eyes. He was clutching at his left forearm and shrank back as I approached. The back of his hand and his forearm were covered with deep scratches, all of them infected. A nurse bathed the arm with antiseptic.

As I lifted him onto a table he screamed with pain. I looked at the ugly swelling of his arm and thought of those at home who had said, 'Leave the Africans alone. They're happy enough as they are.'

The nurse spread old newspapers on the floor. Kefa brought me plaster of Paris bandages. They sank with a gurgle into a dish of water.

The boy laughed as he watched the bubbles rise to the surface. I laughed with him.

'Behold, this is a way of wisdom. This white medicine is particularly strong. As it dries, it hardens. It is as if we were putting a new bone outside your skin until the old bone inside can grow strong and mend.'

The boy hesitated. 'Bwana, does it hurt?'

I looked up at Daudi. He nodded and returned as I was preparing the first bandage.

On the end of the table he put a lump of brown sugar as big as a tennis ball and, smiling broadly, remarked, 'This is the medicine we give to those who make no sound when they are treated.'

The boy clenched his teeth. Gently I lifted the broken arm. Kefa supported it while I put the plaster into position. It stood out in startling whiteness against his black skin. His teeth were still clenched. I put another bandage on, shaped it round the edges and held it for the required five minutes to give it a chance to set.

'Did it hurt?'

'Not yet, Bwana, but have you finished?'

I adjusted the sling around his neck.

'*Kabisa*, completely.'

The boy's hand went out for the sticky lump of sugar. His father walked in. There was an air of cheerfulness that had not been present half-an-hour before.

Kefa stood silent wiping the plaster of Paris from the table.

'Bwana,' he said, 'now I understand what you were telling me this morning. Am I not like a broken arm myself? I only produce pain but when I am strengthened with the power and wisdom of God then the pain goes. If I obey instructions soon I am a useful arm again, not to do my own wishes but rather to do what God wants me to do.'

'*Yoh*,' said the boy's father, 'what's he talking about?'

'Let me explain, Bwana,' said Kefa. 'Behold, there is a chance for me to be really useful to God again …'

A week went by and there was no sign of the boy. The next week he returned, sling intact, but with the plaster strangely soft.

I asked what had happened.

'Behold, Bwana, many of my relations arrived to visit and they all wanted to see this earth of wisdom which changes from power to stone when it is wetted. They all pushed at it with their fingers and scratched it with their nails and behold, Bwana, I have many relations.'

The plaster was off and in coming off pulled some of the hairs on the boy's arm. '*Yoh!*' he gasped. 'It bites.'

I felt along the track of the bone. There opposite the break was a lump where repairs were going on.

Daudi produced more plaster bandages but I waved them aside. 'They're expensive things, Daudi. They're worth about a shilling each. We can't afford to spend more than two or three shillings on a fracture when we have lives to save.'

'Bwana,' said Kefa, 'this boy's arm needs support. What will you do?'

In a dark corner on the top shelf of the cupboard I saw bottles of ether, each enclosed in a wrapper of corrugated cardboard. Taking one of these I put it round his arm. Two thin pieces of sticking plaster held the cardboard in place and the job was complete.

'Leave that on for a week and then the bone inside will be strong – stronger than it's ever been before.'

'True,' agreed Kefa, 'something of the strength from the outside seems to be taken on by the bone inside.'

I looked at him questioningly.

'Bwana, it's true what you said. Ask Jesus to do it and he holds you and holds you firmly. You feel stronger and better and more able to do things. *Yoh*, it was a good story that you told me.'

With a shy smile the boy went outside and returned with a long stick of sugar cane.

'This, Bwana, is my gift to you who helped me greatly.'

I turned to Kefa. 'Have you shown your thankfulness to God for what he's done for you?'

'I had forgotten that part, Bwana.'

Kefa had ups and downs but became one of our most trusted and effective helpers.

10
Wax

He was extremely tall and extremely miserable. He stood in front of me and shook his head, his eyes on the ground. I took stock of him. The burn scar in the centre of his forehead and his tremendously long ear lobes proclaimed him a member of the local tribe. But when I greeted him in Chigogo he took not the slightest notice.

'*Mbukwa*,' I repeated. 'Good day.'

He said nothing.

I raised my voice. '*Mbukwa*.'

'*Twee*,' said Daudi. 'Not a word. Try him in Swahili, Bwana.'

I did. '*Jambo. Jambo! Jambo!*'

Daudi smiled.

Then I tried a couple of other languages. '*Kamweni*,' the greeting of the Wahehe – the neighbouring tribe. Again no reply. '*Mwangaluka*,' I greeted using the language of the Mountains of the Moon.

This seemed at last to produce results. He looked up but there was no light of comprehension in his eyes. He slouched off, sat down on a three-legged stool, put his head in his hands and groaned.

I had an idea and taking a piece of paper I wrote: 'Why are you so sad?'

I handed it to him and was not reassured when he held it upside down and looked at it glumly. I felt we'd reached a deadlock.

I was racking my brains for some new line of attack, when the miserable figure suddenly threw the paper to the ground and said firmly, *'Sinosuma kusoma, hamba kuhilika hamba cinji, nili bwete.* I can't read and I can't hear. I'm worthless.'

He rose wearily and I grasped his shoulder and pushed him back. Daudi brought the ear examination tray and pulling my stethoscope from my pocket I put the ear part into his ears and yelled down the chest piece. 'Can you hear now?'

A slow smile spread over his face. *'Yoh*, Bwana, that's better. *Heeh*, I can hear. Then surely I'm not bewitched.' He seemed struck by an idea. 'Bwana,' he cried excitedly, 'I'll give you a cow for this thing.' He waved the stethoscope hopefully in the air and then caressed its rubber tubes.

I tried to make him grasp that I could help him to hear but in his enthusiasm he seemed to think that I was holding out for a higher price. He proceeded to bargain. 'Bwana, I'll pay a cow and a goat – a fat one.'

I shook my head and opened a little black box that Daudi handed me. Adjusting a trumpet-shaped instrument fitted with a minute electric bulb that gave a clear view into his ear, I motioned my deaf friend to keep still. He was suspicious. I put the stethoscope back in place and bellowed, 'I'm going to look into your ears. Look in front and keep your head still.'

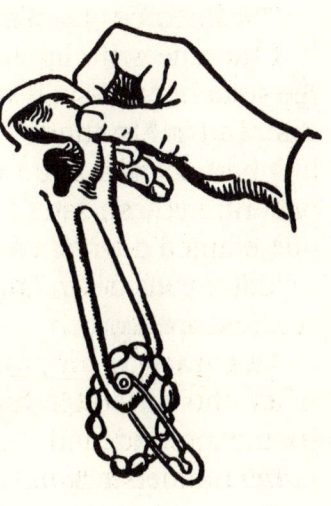

The answer was a beaming smile and the reply, '*Yeh!* Bwana, I can hear a noise like bees swarming.'

Daudi chuckled. In desperation I grasped our patient by the ear lobe and peered in. The whole ear was blocked with tar-like wax and I saw some remnants of grass.

'*Muganga*, the witchdoctor,' remarked Daudi looking in his turn. The other ear was even worse and had obviously been prodded with a thorn.

'How long have you been deaf?' I shouted.

'No, Bwana,' said the deaf man.

Daudi yelled at the top of his voice repeating the question. The man sadly shook his head. It seemed hopeless.

'Syringe out those ears, Daudi, and then we'll have some fun.'

I went back to my work and about an hour later I came back to find Daudi still syringing. There was a grim line about his mouth and the patient had a pathetic look in his eye.

'What's up, Daudi? Things not so good?'

'*Kah*,' said Daudi, 'Bwana, here I am squirting warm water through the syringe and not a spot of wax. *Kah!*'

'Try the other ear, Daudi.'

I saw the grinning face of Mboga, hugely enjoying the joke. I called out to him and the last I saw was Daudi sitting in the shade while his junior set to work filling and emptying the syringe into the ear of our patient. An hour later I returned to find a weary male nurse and a depressed patient.

'Can you hear anything?' I tested with the stethoscope again.

'Yes, Bwana.'

'I'm going to put medicine into your ears to soften the wax in there.'

He nodded his head so enthusiastically that the stethoscope came out. Nothing daunted he shook my hand vigorously and said I was his father and mother.

I went into the dispensary and wrote a prescription. Daudi read it over, took up measures and deftly mixed the contents of sundry bottles. He neatly wrote a label, stuck it on and presented me with the bottle and an ear dropper.

Our patient watched everything with wide eyes. As I filled the dropper he opened his mouth. Once again the stethoscope came into use and soon the drops were in his ears. I explained that next day, when the wax had softened a bit, we would syringe again and then we could hope for results.

I called the staff together and using this case as an example, set them to work to demonstrate ear treatment. Everyone sat watching while Mboga prepared an ear tray. He set out three bowls, one with sterile water, one with peroxide and one with cotton wool. There was also the syringe and a kidney dish.

'Bwana,' said Mboga, 'this dish has warm water in it and bicarb soda. This is for ordinary syringing.'

'Why is the water warm?' I asked a junior nurse. She gaped, shook her head and no one seemed to know. So we syringed her ears with cold water. After the third treatment she said, 'Yoh! I feel giddy.' She staggered and almost fell.

It was a demonstration no one was likely to forget. 'Why use a kidney-shaped dish?' was the next question.

Daudi's answer was eloquent. He held a round bowl to the neck of the nurse and then the kidney-shaped one. 'See,' he cried. 'It saves the water from being spilled down the sick one's neck.'

Next morning I peered into the patient's ear again. The wax looked brownish and soft. Daudi appeared with his half-kerosene tin of hot water, his syringe, a kidney bowl and some cotton wool swabs.

He led the deaf man over to the tomato garden, sat him down on a stool and loaded up. A group of small boys stood round to watch. With a twinkle in his eye Daudi squirted a syringeful into their faces. They gasped and fled.

The deaf man laughed loudly and said in a megaphone-like voice, '*Yoh*, behold, that medicine moved things.'

Still smiling, Daudi grasped the man's ear, put the syringe nozzle in position and squirted. The first attempt did little but the second one was coloured and faintly brown.

'It's coming, Bwana,' called Daudi.

And come it did. With a yell the deaf man pulled his ear from Daudi's grasp, knocked stool and bowl flying and danced triumphantly among the tomato plants.

Mboga protested loudly, prodded him with a broom and shouted, '*Koh*, be careful of my garden!'

'*Yoh*,' said the dancer with a grin that was at once wide and broad. 'Don't bother to raise your voice for me now. Was I not rejoicing because once again I can hear?'

'Sit down, then,' ordered Daudi. 'You've got two ears to be fixed up. Let me finish the work.'

He carefully picked up a black mass that had come from the ear and showed me a plug of rubbish which was the end result of witchdoctor's treatment. In a few moments the whole action was repeated.

Daudi peered into the ear and said triumphantly, 'Clear. I can see the drum.'

In his hand were the wax plugs. Daudi believed in the value of attack. He held them under the nose of our patient.

'There, don't you ever tell me you can't understand what sin is. Here is a picture of it and it tells its own story.'

The poor fellow gasped. '*Yoh*, that only stopped me from hearing your words.'

'True,' said Daudi, 'but sin stops you from hearing and understanding God. Now that your ears work it is your responsibility to reply when people talk to you. Behold, now you must hear the words of God when he says, "The wages of sin is death but the gift of God is eternal life through Jesus Christ."'

'*Yoh*, Bwana Daudi, this is hard to understand.'

'Well, stay close and you will hear more. If you go to your home more wax will come and soon you will be deaf again. Stay near to us here and we can remove the wax each time it appears.'

'Behold,' said Mboga, 'is that not like sin? If you go far from the Lord Jesus, soon you lose the hearing of your soul. But stay close to where he can help you, then all is well.'

'Behold, I will stay,' said the once-deaf man.

'*Swanu*, good,' replied Daudi, 'for you have a new responsibility. Didn't Jesus say, "He who has ears to hear, let him use them"?'

'*Eeeeh*,' said the smiling man who could now hear, 'you have taken the blockage from my ears and opened new thoughts for my mind.'

'That's what we're here for,' said Daudi.

11

Pneumonia

It doesn't often rain in Central Tanzania, but when it does it pours.

Heavy drops of the tropical thunderstorm beat on the tin roof of the hospital. The thunder crashed alarmingly and the lightning, for a split second, turned the intense darkness into bright white light. The hurricane lantern on the window ledge was a mere glimmer. By it I watched a small boy lying in a cot made from packing cases.

He was sitting propped up with pillows, if you can call unbleached calico filled with dry grass a pillow. He was covered by a cotton blanket and a patchwork quilt. His life was in the balance – pneumonia treated by all the devilry of the witchdoctor. I expected the crisis that night. The boy stirred restlessly and I saw a large white patch on that quilt with the inscription: 'With love from the Sunday School of St. Luke's'.

It was a splendidly made quilt. How I would have liked all the people who had stitched so industriously making that colourful piece of bedding to be with me for an hour. And suddenly as it had begun the storm ended. A hyena started its weird laughter behind the hospital fence.

From somewhere in the room came snoring which certainly wasn't that of a child. I went to investigate and there, under the bed with her feet sticking out, was the grandmother of one of the patients. She should not have been there but at that hour of the night I realised I would only wake the whole hospital if I attempted to do anything about it.

Once again the hyena howled. The boy propped up on the pillows muttered and half-opened his eyes. It was two o'clock in the morning and time to give him an injection. The rain started again. I saw a round mark appear underneath the roof in one corner. It spread down and soon an ugly reddish-brown streak spread down the whitewash of the wall. The fiercely-driven rain had torn its way through the mud bricks. I knew this would mean more bricks to be made after the storm.

Suddenly there was a tremendous flash of lightning followed immediately by a clap of thunder. The whole place seemed to shake.

The boy opened his eyes and screamed. I went over and quietened him.

'It's all right, Mtoto. It's only a bit of thunder.'

He clung to my hand. Gently I gave him an injection.

Within minutes the medicine took its effect and the boy lost the look of strain and slipped back to sleep.

The mud streak on the wall now extended almost to the floor.

The African night nurse came in. '*Hongo*, Mwendwa. I think he'll sleep all right now. He has had his medicine and an injection to bring sleep.'

'*Kah!* He will sleep here, Bwana, but he would not have done so at home. He's only a small boy!'

'But he would have had a blanket, or something to cover him?'

'No, Bwana, he would just lie on the ground.'

'But if they saw that he was as sick as he is, perhaps they would throw a cow skin over him.'

'But, Bwana, many children die when they have this disease. Do not our people say they have been stabbed by some evil spirit? The children have pain when they breathe and our Wagogo folk think that an evil spirit comes and stabs them in the chest. They breathe very fast. They cough. Their strength goes and often they die. Then all the family wail because one of their tribe has passed over to their ancestors.'

I slipped a thermometer under the child's arm. The temperature was normal. Thankfully I left the hospital and walked down a puddle-studded path. There was hardly a cloud in a starlit sky. Thunderstorms come and go with amazing rapidity in the rainy season.

I was dog-tired and slumped into bed after a hasty mosquito hunt. It seemed to me that I had barely touched the pillow when a voice outside called, 'Bwana, come at once. The child with pneumonia is at the point of death.' There was an urgency in Mwendwa's voice.

I dragged on clothes and raced to the hospital. The child's bed was empty. Back along the path the grandmother staggered, clutching the boy in her arms.

I arrived in time to snatch our small patient from the exhausted woman.

'Let me carry him,' came Mboga's voice through the darkness.

Adders and a collection of snakes often chose to sleep on that pathway but that night none of us had a thought for reptiles.

In the ward I injected a strong stimulant. In a matter of minutes Mtoto's eyes flickered.

Mhutila, the water carrier, had made his first journey of the day from the wells carrying two kerosene tins full of water – one suspended on each end of a pole across his muscular shoulders. Mhutila was just the one to take the grandmother home. He would look after her kindly but firmly.

I put my head through the window.

'Mhutila.' He came over. 'I have here a woman who does not obey the words of the hospital. Will you take her home and see that she stays there?'

'Bwana,' chuckled the water carrier, 'it will give me considerable joy.'

Somewhat noisily the grandmother went home.

Three days later when I saw my pneumonia patient sitting comfortably in bed there was a great change for the better. The child was still coughing but the disease was well and truly in check.

When we were having our morning prayers in the outpatients' room, I saw a boy's head appear above the window sill. Daudi was talking about Mponyi, the healer. He told of Jesus who healed men's bodies and who made all the difference to men's souls.

'*Yoh*,' said Mtoto, 'was it he you were talking to when I nearly died?'

'Yes, Mtoto, it was.'

'He answered you, Bwana.'

'He did, indeed. He cares for us both very much.'

12
Sore Thumb

Along a winding path showing white against the red soil, came a stalwart figure moving at a brisk pace. He carried over his shoulders two large cone-shaped baskets.

'*Yoh!*' said Mboga. 'Here comes Matayo. He brings joy to our tongues. There are no pawpaws better than his in this part of the country. If ever there is *mpiligazi*, a hard worker, it's this man Matayo.'

'Words of truth, Bwana,' agreed Mboga. 'He lives right over there.' He pointed with his chin towards a granite boulder-covered mountain side. 'At Chikuyu, the place of fig trees, he has a splendid garden, and *kumbe*, he works hard. Not only that, Bwana, but he is the teacher in that village. He will not receive one cent for the work that he does. He prefers to work in his garden and sell his fruit.'

'Well that suits me. When Matayo comes and sells me his fruit it means that we have all the pawpaws that we need. Believe me, Mboga, it's important to eat as much fruit and vegetables as we possibly can.'

'*Koh*, Bwana, if you have *wugali,* porridge, that's all that's required. Are not our people well-developed?'

'No, Mboga, they're not. Look at that child playing out there in the sun.' The little fellow was obviously suffering from rickets. 'He should have been given milk as well as porridge. He needs to have a mixed diet, not merely porridge as is the custom here.

'*Koh*, Bwana, but the cows here don't give much milk.'

'That's true, but you ought to give the children every drop you can get.'

Matayo was coming close now. There was a haggard look about my favourite gardener. He took the ancient hat from his head. As he did so I saw his right hand was tied up with an old piece of rag.

'*Mbukwa*, Matayo, how are you?'

'*Eeeh*, Bwana, I haven't the smallest bit of joy.'

'That doesn't sound like you, Matayo. What happened?'

'*Koh*, Bwana, my hand! *Heeeh*, for days and days it's been aching and aching and I can't sleep. *Kumbe*, it's an awful feeling so I have come to you.'

'Good, we'll see what we can do. Leave one basket of pawpaws here and we'll go up to the hospital.'

I produced a shilling which was the price of one of these splendid baskets of luscious fruit. Matayo rummaged with his left hand in the second basket and pulled out six green limes and presented them to me.

'These are for you, and two corn cobs.'

Now corn does not usually grow at that time of the year but Matayo had planted a few grains and had carefully tended them knowing how much I liked sweet corn.

Carefully carrying his other basket of pawpaws he came with me to the hospital. In a few minutes the patients and nurses had bought all his fruit and were sitting in the shade enjoying them.

I sat Matayo down on a box, shook down a thermometer and put it under his tongue. No sooner was it in place than he wanted to talk.

'Will you be quiet, Matayo? You must keep that under your tongue for a few minutes and then we'll hear the story you have to tell.'

I felt his pulse at the same time. I looked at the silver line of mercury. He had a high fever.

Removing the piece of cloth wrapped round his hand I saw the cause of his trouble. At the base of his thumb, the normal swollen portion of his hand was three times its normal size. I touched it. It was acutely tender. Then I tried to move the thumb and again intense pain. I examined the other fingers, the palm of his hand, his elbow and I felt the glands under his arm.

'Matayo, we can help you all right but you're going to be in hospital for perhaps a week.'

'Koh, Bwana, who will look after my garden?'

'Who will look after your hand if anything goes

93

wrong? What value is there in a man whose hand will not work, especially if it's his right hand?'

He shook his head. 'Bwana, your words are wise. I would like you to give me the pills that take away pain though. Behold, it throbs with strength.'

'Matayo, there is little value in just giving you pills to take away the throbbing feelings. The pills will stop the pain for a while but they would not stop the damage that is going on inside your hand. Unless I remove from your hand all the trouble that is hidden there, behold, you will have a hand that has no value to you at all.'

Daudi was standing beside me. 'Bwana, I don't suppose Matayo has been able to do any work for many days.'

'*Koh*,' said Matayo, 'for three days now I have done nothing.'

'When did you last have anything to eat?'

'Bwana, I have not been able to eat.'

'Nothing at all, not even a pawpaw?'

'Oh, well, Bwana, two or three of those.'

I looked at the large fruit and saw what he thought was 'nothing at all' was not quite the same as my idea of it.

'Here, take this pill for the pain and rest a while.'

About four hours later he came to the operating theatre. Daudi opened a bottle of anaesthetic and everyone was scrubbed up and ready.

'Bwana, before you give me the medicine of sleep show me what you're going to do.'

I took his good hand and showed it to him.

'Are you going to cut me?'

'Yes.' Holding his palm upward and turning it round I looked at the back of the hand. 'If you cut into the palm of the hand, even if it's only a little bit, it's dangerous. You might cut nerves, you might cut arteries, so you go to the back of the hand and find the bone of the first finger. You make a little cut there and you take out the trouble that is in the hand through that hole. In that way there is no danger of hurting the nerves of the hand.'

'*Koh*, if I'd been doing it, I would have made a cut in the closest part.'

'Yes, Matayo, you would and you would have done a lot of damage. You see my medical books tell me exactly what is the best way to do it. Many doctors give their experience. That is how we know what to do.'

'*Heeeh*, Bwana, there is always a right way and a wrong way.'

'Truly. You remember what Solomon said in his book of Proverbs? Did he not say there is a way that seems right to a man but in the end it leads to death. You see, you could ruin your hand if you went your own way. Let us follow the ways of wisdom.'

Before he had the anaesthetic we asked Almighty God to help us to follow the way of wisdom not only in surgery but in life.

I started the anaesthetic and a few minutes later he was breathing deeply. In a matter of seconds the abscess in his hand was open.

'*Kumbe*,' said Daudi, 'that will soon be better.'

'*Eheh*,' said Matayo next morning, 'that is better, Bwana.'

The swelling went down slowly but surely.

Before long Matayo with his hand bandaged and with a pot of ointment in his large cone-shaped basket was wending his way home. He walked through the baobab grove to the little CMS school on the side of the granite boulder-studded hill – the place where the fig trees were. I knew that the people of that village would hear again that the only way to everlasting life was through Jesus Christ, the Son of God.

13
Beer and Burns

'*Ndio*, yes,' said Daudi, 'we had a famine last year. The crops were bad and everybody prayed to God. They were very sorry for their sins when their stomachs were empty. But this year the rains were good, the crops were excellent, everybody's grain bins were full of corn and few people even bothered to remember God.

'Instead of storing up corn for an emergency they spent much time brewing beer. Behold, these days the village reeks of home brew. Before long we will be very busy at the hospital. Night after night men will break other men's heads when they're drunk. We will spend hours operating – repairing damage done by a man full of a beer with a *knobkerrie* in his hand.

'*Yoh!*' he spat forcefully.

'I take it therefore, Daudi, that you don't agree with those who drink much beer?'

97

Daudi looked at me. 'There was a time, Bwana, when I drank a lot. They call it food and truly, it is food for headaches and heartaches. *Heeeh.*'

He spat again and I could see that he was about to break into a further tirade against what the locals called *wujimbi*. But at that moment we heard children's voices. It was not the usual laughing chatter of little people. There was fear and urgency in the sound.

'The Bwana's here,' said one of them. And I heard, '*Hodi, hodi*? May I come in?'

Two small girls were on the verandah. The taller of them was seven. On her back she carried a two-year-old boy who was screaming with pain. Her smaller sister was trying to get him safely to the ground. The girl who had been carrying him looked utterly weary and both the sisters were in distress.

Carefully I lifted the baby down and put him on our examination table. He was covered in blisters – red raw in places where the skin had rubbed off while he was being carried to hospital.

Both the little girls squatted on the floor. Tears ran down their faces. Daudi produced a tube of tannic acid jelly while I gave the burnt child medicine to control his pain.

I asked the girl, 'What is your name?'

'Marita, Bwana.'

'Tell me, Marita, how did he come to get burned like that?'

'Bwana, he was scalded when a clay pot of *wujimbi* broke as he was crawling on the ground and the boiling beer went all over him.'

'*Koh*,' said Daudi, 'why did they send you with the child?'

The five-year-old sister whose name we discovered was Pepetua answered like a shot out of a gun. '*Koh*, were they not all drunk?'

'What?' queried Daudi. 'Drunk at this hour of the morning?'

'*Yoh*,' said Marita. 'Have they recovered from what they drank last night?'

'Do we not go to the village school at Ndebwe?' said Pepetua. 'Have we not drunk the medicine of the hospital for our coughs? So we said, "We will take him to the Bwana. He will help".'

'But,' broke in Daudi, 'will not your relations be angry?'

'*Yoh*,' replied Marita, 'will he not die unless you help with speed?'

While we were speaking, treatment was given to the small child. I am always concerned about burns in children. There are few more dangerous accidents.

'This is a case for a blood transfusion, Daudi. Go down to the house and talk to the relations. Take the chief with you if you wish. Make all the trouble in the world as long as you get half-a-dozen people willing to give their blood.'

An hour later Daudi arrived by himself. 'Bwana, all that the children said was true. They are all drunk, hopelessly drunk. Not one of them was even able to walk and they all refuse to come.'

'Bwana,' said Marita, 'can't we help? Do we not love our little brother?'

'Listen children, what we want is some blood from some well person to run into your little brother's veins.'

'Bwana,' said a teenaged schoolgirl, 'You can have some of mine. I'm not frightened.'

'Bwana,' said Daudi, 'try mine.'

'We can't do it, Daudi. I once gave some of my blood on a job like this and I was dizzy all the time I was operating. We can't be the blood bank as well as the hospital staff. There are other lives depending on us.'

The blood donor girl behaved like a veteran. She didn't flinch while I made tests nor when I took half-a-litre of blood from her arm. But as I bandaged up that arm she suddenly fainted. We put her into a bed next to the boy and with Marita and Pepetua she watched open-eyed as we ran the blood into the injured child's arm.

Halfway through this proceeding I heard a murmur of voices outside. Daudi was laying down the law to somebody in no uncertain terms.

'*Yoh*,' whispered Pepetua, 'it is the voice of my father.' She huddled up in a corner. 'He's *kali sana*, very fierce. He beats us when he's drunk.'

Daudi came to the door. 'The father's here, Bwana,' he said in English. 'He's almost sober but don't speak with him. He's not worth the words.'

Over his shoulder peered the unkempt head of an African I knew quite well. He had been a quarryman and had worked for me when we built the hospital wards.

'Bwana,' said Daudi again, speaking in English, 'when he speaks to you, don't reply. Let him realise how great is the wrong he has done.'

It was a chastened man to whom I spoke later that evening.

'Nhete, you have two grand little daughters. Marita is as brave as a lion. They have saved your son's life while you snored like a hog.'

'*Koh*,' grunted Daudi, his tone oozing disgust.

'But Bwana, I didn't know.'

'Of course you didn't,' said Daudi. 'You didn't care. *Kah!* Get out! Don't let us see you till tomorrow. You reek of beer.'

I went back to my little patient. He was out of danger.

Next morning Daudi had an idea. 'Bwana, let us go and visit that part of the country where these people live. I have doubts.'

So had I.

We walked that evening through a belt of cactus to the village. 'There's a man here,' Daudi told me, 'his name is Tumbo.'

'Why, he was one of the masons who worked with us.'

'Yes, Bwana, and I have heard that his wife Abigaili makes large quantities of beer at his house and I think it was his beer that made these people drunk.'

At that moment we came out on a clearing and in front of us, smiling blandly, was Tumbo. '*Mbukwa*, Bwana.'

I greeted him and then got straight down to business.

'Tumbo, I hear you've been brewing beer.'

'Bwana, I? Your chief mason brew beer? Me? No, Bwana.'

'*Koh*, you are full of words.'

'Bwana, if you don't believe me, come and look. Search my house.'

'*Kah*,' snorted Daudi in English, 'did they not know we were coming? Is not everything hidden?'

'I thought of that, Daudi, and I've brought my torch – the big one.'

Tumbo had already reached the door of his house and was standing aside for us to enter. 'Search, Bwana. Everywhere. You will not find any beer in my house.'

The beam of light probed every corner of that dim mud-roofed, mud-walled, mud-floored African house. I saw the cowskins they used for beds. I almost stepped on a hen's nest containing four eggs. There was a pile of straw in a corner which Daudi moved.

'*Heh*,' smirked Tumbo, 'is there beer there? Look under the eggs, Bwana.'

But I noticed he walked past a large wickerwork grain bin. Stopping I shone the light into this.

'Just grain, Bwana, only grain. Nothing else.'

Daudi prodded the millet with his stick and a hollow sound resulted.

'*Yoh*,' I gasped in amazement, 'what's that?'

'Oh, nothing,' said Tumbo, 'nothing at all. Nothing at all.'

Daudi scraped the grain away and revealed two large clay pots full of beer.

'*Kah!*' shouted Daudi, his eyebrows almost in his hairline. Tumbo shook his head. 'Now that shows you what people will do. What a shabby trick, hiding their pots of beer in my house.'

'You really did not know those pots were there?' I asked.

'No,' said Tumbo, 'I had no idea. They had no business whatsoever to put them there.'

'And you don't want the beer?'

'No,' said Tumbo, 'certainly not.'

'*Kah*,' ground out Daudi, 'it if doesn't belong to you and you don't want it, then you won't mind tipping it out?'

'*Er*, no,' said Tumbo, carrying on bravely, 'it will teach them – er – a good lesson, whoever put it there.'

A minute later the air reeked with the smell of spilt beer. As we walked back to the hospital Daudi said, 'It's true, Bwana, that your sin will find you out. But it seems tragic when because of your sin other people suffer, especially children.'

14
Fair, Fat and Forty

Daudi was giving a lecture on primus stoves.

'Now watch.'

He got to work with the pump.

'As surely as …' At that moment kerosene squirted out through the burner and a sheet of flame shot into the air.

One of his listeners, in his excitement, fell backwards off his three-legged stood. There was a hiss as Daudi opened the valve and the flames died down.

'Watch out for fire,' said Daudi, 'and be careful not to be in too great a hurry. Remember the Swahili proverb, "Hurry, hurry has no blessing." Wait until the machine is hot, until the blue flame is small, then pump – not before. Go gently and do not only go gently when you're using a machine like the primus but when you deal with people. Do not let your anger flare up. God's book says, "A soft answer turns away wrath."'

He waited this time until the flame was small, pumped gently and the machine worked.

'Call the doctor at once.' The nurse on duty was in a high state of excitement. 'They've brought a cow, a good cow.'

I looked through the window and there was a rather skinny bull. All bulls are cows to the Wagogo who think of them as part of a dowry price or as an *asante*, thank offering, for an operation.

'*Yoh*,' said Daudi, 'is it the gift of a chief?'

'It is the gift of a chief – the Great One from right over there.' She pointed with her chin and her voice became high-pitched showing the chief came from a considerable distance from the hospital.

There was a giggle. 'He's fat, extremely fat, and he's making a dreadful noise. His *karani*, his clerk, says that he will give the Bwana the cow straight away if only he can stop the pain.'

Daudi already had the chief lying on two forms put side by side under the shade of a pepper tree. Soon we were surrounded by an interested crowd.

As I walked up one of the chief's helpers said, '*Yoh*, he's a weight. Did it not take six of us to carry him? Nhembo, the elephant, is his relation and, Bwana, does he make a noise! He says, *u-k-k-k-k-k!* and *e-e-e-e-e-!* and then he screams and froths at the mouth.'

'Does he bite his tongue?' asked Daudi.

'*N'go*, is it not the work of *mapepo*, of evil spirits.'

'But,' said another of the bearers, 'he draws his knees up, clasps his hands over his stomach and groans and the noises he makes …' He shook his head and I grinned thinking of what I had learned in my medical school.

Fair, fat and forty – a classical description of someone with gall-stones.

I examined him. He certainly was fat. He probably was forty but his skin colour was distinctly strange. His eyes did not shine white as they normally do from a black face. There he lay with the crowd looking on. When I tried to shoo them away, Daudi said, 'It's all right, Bwana, he likes this.' So I continued my examination in what looked like a football scrum.

My fingers quested in the rolls of his ample midriff. When they reached the area under his ribs on the right side, he let out a yell that sent children scuttling for cover.

'There we are, Daudi. Look at his eyes. They're yellow. See where the pain is? He has gall-stones.'

I wrote out orders for a special injection. Daudi hurried to prepare it. We carried our bulky patient to the ward and I was amused to see Elisha, the carpenter, bring six petrol boxes to support the frame of the bed.

With a grunt the unfortunate chief sank down on the bed and with a grunt the ropes of the mattress stretched to their limit.

Daudi appeared with a syringe. 'Now, Great One,' he said, 'your pain will be conquered quickly.'

For five minutes the sick man lay there making all the doleful sounds imaginable and then they gradually eased into sighs of relief. He even attempted to sit up.

'Chief,' I urged, 'quietly now. I have merely covered up your pain.'

'I don't care, Bwana. It's gone.'

'But it will come back again.'

Turning to his followers he said, 'Give the Bwana the cow.'

The words were no sooner out of his mouth than a secret signal went from Daudi and I learnt afterwards that the unfortunate animal was skilfully butchered. The hospital staff were afraid that the chief might change his mind.

I ordered various treatments including a hot brick wrapped in an old piece of blanket – our local equivalent of a hot water bottle – and I left my now-beaming patient with this burden reposing elegantly along his middle.

Daudi had everything organised. As I went outside the ward I found Samson cutting off lumps of steak and Kefa had a hindquarter over his shoulders. The nurses had all demanded their particular bit while the schoolgirls were hastily collecting firewood for a bonfire and the Tanzanian modification of a barbecue.

Suddenly they all burst into song, one of their favourite cultivating songs with its rhythm making you almost hear the hoes digging deep into moist soil. They didn't sing it once but half a dozen times altering the words to fit in with the various bits of meat that they had.

As I walked home in the sunset I could hear the enthusiastic song. I watched the crows flying overhead and heard boys driving home the cattle. A few lonely-looking cornstalks of last year's crop stuck up here and there in the dryness and brownness of the plains that stretched to the foothills of the Great Rift Wall. It was not completely dark.

I changed my shorts for a thick pair of mosquito-proof trousers and long leather boots that protected my ankles. There were at least a hundred eager people waiting for the fire to be lit. They had sticks of all lengths and each one had his own little bit of meat that we would roast for him. On a long piece of fencing wire was the main morsel of the evening put so that it would swing to and fro like a pendulum along the length of the fire.

I struck a match, lighted the dry grass and in a minute the flames were leaping, the meat sizzling and the crowd singing. Song followed song. Stories like Aesop's fables were told until a voice called 'Cooked!'

For quite a time there was silence broken only by appreciative noises and the sound of teeth dealing with tough meat.

In the middle of it came a call. 'The Chief is gripped again with strong pain.'

I was quickly at his side. Another injection stilled his agony. He sighed with relief but I shook my head. 'Great One, make no mistake. Injections only cover up the pain. We must get rid of the cause of it. It is a matter of difficulty.'

He nodded his head. 'Help me, Bwana. Help me with strength.'

An hour after dawn everything was ready for the operation. By noon it was all over. The Chief was pain free and the cause of his trouble, a gall-stone the size of a marble, sat safely in a convenient bottle.

15
The Bad Shepherd

'Over there,' whispered Daudi.

In the starlight we saw two vague shadows in the middle of the dry river bed. The moon came from behind the cloud.

'Look, Bwana, *mabisi*, hyenas. They have something down there in the creek. My nose tells me that it has been dead for a long time.'

Daudi gripped a knobbed stick and I picked up a large stone. The hyenas howled eerily and slunk away into the darkness. I focussed my flashlight on the stinking carcass.

'*Hongo*, Daudi, some boy will be in trouble for being a careless shepherd. In one of the local villages not far from here there will be one who will hear angry words from his father.'

Daudi nodded. 'It is the work of the *mudimi*, the shepherd to care for his sheep and to protect them from wild animals.'

Next morning Daudi came to me. 'Bwana, you remember the hyenas and the dead sheep?'

'I do indeed.'

Daudi went on. 'The boy who was the shepherd is in trouble. His father was furious and beat him. The boy ran away from his father's house and went to the *kaya* of his relations on the far side of the swamp – a considerable safari. Night came as he travelled so he slept in an old hut that had no door. Before dawn *mbisi*, the hyena came to that hut and tore at his arm. The boy fought for his life and managed to drive the scavenger away.'

'Was it an ugly bite, Daudi?'

'Yes, Bwana, and the boy had strong pain but he managed to struggle to the place of his relations. They took him to the medicine man who said they must find the reason for the anger of the spirits. Medicine was made and a charm put round the young shepherd's neck.'

'That did little to help?'

'Truly, Bwana, and behold his condition turned to blood poisoning. When they feared that he would die they brought him here to the hospital. The news now is that he has high fever. He talks with wild delirium.'

When we examined the damaged arm it was clear that the filthy jaws of hyena and witchdoctor's medicine had landed the boy dangerously close to death. In our emergency cupboard we had no antibiotic medicine that could deal with his problem. Quickly we got him to hospital where we had a long difficult day. His temperature was critical.

At second cock crow he awoke in wild delirium, but soon after dawn, Daudi reported, 'He's considerably better but during the night he talked wild words of small wisdom. He had much sadness because of the things he did not do when he should have been looking after his father's sheep.'

'Was it the beating his father gave him?'

'No, Bwana, the main trouble was that the other herdsmen jeered at him with many words. "You're not a good shepherd. You don't watch your sheep. For this reason the *mapepo*, the spirits attack you."'

That evening Mwendwa came to my office. 'He's out of danger, Bwana. I saw his lips moving and I heard him say, "I feel better but my stomach calls for food".'

But it took weeks for his arm to heal. One day he sat in the shade of the pepper trees while Yakobo bandaged his arm which was slowly improving. I came to look for progress and we started talking about shepherds.

I told him how Jesus had said, 'I am the good shepherd and I know those that are mine and my sheep know me. I am giving my life for the sake of the sheep and I have other sheep who do not belong to this fold. I will lead them also and they will hear my voice. So there will be one flock and one shepherd.'

'He said he would look after his sheep. He would keep them from the wild animals. He would not let any thief steal them from him.'

They listened intently and then the hyena bite boy said, 'Bwana, I was not a good shepherd.'

'*Kumbe*, you can understand what it means to sheep who couldn't trust you. Jesus wants you to be one of his sheep. He will never let you down as you let down your sheep.'

'Bwana, have I not been close to those gates through which no one comes back?'

I nodded. 'You speak the truth.'

'Bwana, surely I needed to have Jesus with me then.'

'Truly, but you need him more while you're walking along the path here and now.'

'Bwana, I know I need him.'

'Well, what are you going to do?'

'Do you think, Bwana, if I asked him, he will take me to be one of his sheep?'

I nodded. 'There's absolutely no doubt about it.'

16
Hyena Bite

The only form of lighting we had in our jungle hospital was that useful device, the hurricane lantern. I hung it on a nail driven into one of the rafters of the ward

roof. A cheerful young man named Ngoma greeted me as I bent over his leg to change the dressing on a skin graft. This would normally have been a job for earlier in the day but unexpected emergencies had arrived at the hospital. One of them was a hyena bite.

The scavenger had attacked the gardener, Matayo, and his arm was badly damaged. Now he lay in the bed behind me propped up on pillows. He was completely out of his anaesthetic and taking interest in things. Beside his bed on a locker, which not long before had been a kerosene box, were two large white pills and a three-litre bottle of water.

'Matayo, I want you to chew those pills and drink that water – every drop of it. You must drink one bottleful twice a day.'

'*Hongo*, Bwana, how am I to drink from so large a bottle with one of my arms tied up?'

'Look beside you. There is a long glass tube. Put that in the bottle and suck through it.' He proceeded to do so with gusto.

I scrubbed my hands thoroughly in a dish that once had been part of a kerosene tin and proceeded to do the dressing. Ngoma was in his early twenties. On his leg had been an ulcer as big as your hand. We treated it for a long time then one day I took bits of skin from the other leg and grafted them onto the ulcer. It was one of those cases where you would greatly appreciate the best type of equipment. However, ancient mosquito netting soaked in liquid paraffin was the best that we could manage and his leg had been carefully bandaged.

I removed those bandages bathing the leg with special care. Ngoma leaned forward taking a keen interest in my surgical efforts. His relations, one of them a witchdoctor, sneered at the idea of man's skin being taken from one leg and put on the other. The story of this operation had gone right through the village and Ngoma was all keenness to see the result.

With my forceps I removed the bandage bit by bit. Finally when it was all coiled up in a dish the wound lay exposed. There, looking like islands on a map, were the skin grafts. They had taken splendidly and would make that ulcer heal up in three weeks instead of perhaps three months.

I explained to him how it all worked.

'*Koh*' said Ngoma. 'This is a repair work of cunning, Bwana.'

Matayo, the gardener, nodded his head. 'Truly, it is a repair work of great interest, like a gardener moving a plant from one garden to another. *Heeeh*, they do things of wisdom at the hospital.'

He lifted his hand to his ear lobe which once had been so big that you could easily have put a tennis ball in the hole that had been stretched in the lobe. Now it was a small thing – so small that you could barely force a matchstick through.

'Behold, I did not think it was possible that the Bwana could give me back the ears shaped as they were in my youth.'

He had come to me two years before saying he had decided to turn from his heathen ways to serve God. He wanted to indicate this to all his tribesfolk by having his ear lobes reduced in size. In the days when he was not interested in God's ways he had boasted considerably about those ears and he thought it would be a good way to show his change of mind if he had them trimmed.

He was amazed when I told him there was no need to do that for in the operating theatre I could make him a new ear lobe which would be like his old one. I achieved this with a little bit of surgical fancy work and a small amount of local anaesthetic. Matayo carefully checked everything I did with a couple of mirrors. His amazement was great when he saw them appear as they now were.

With his one good hand he took out the New Testament in his own language.

'Bwana, let me read you a verse that is special to me.'

As I put a further dressing on the leg ulcer he read, '"Repent, therefore, and turn to God so that he will forgive your sin".'

'I repented and when my ears were fixed did I not try to turn round and walk God's way?'

'You did. But did you find it easy?'

'*Heeeh*,' he smiled, 'did I not find it difficult. But had I not God's book here and could I not talk to him day and night whenever I wanted to? Was he not my father and my chief and my Saviour?'

I thought of those words as I walked home over the plains through the darkness of the East African night, listening to hyenas howling round the place and the yelping of the jackals. In the thornbush beyond the hospital I could hear a grunting roar which might have been lion or baboon.

A week later I was back at that ward. Matayo lay in bed. He looked ghastly. His arm had given all the trouble that you could imagine and he had lost a lot of blood. I was giving him a blood transfusion. The blood donor was the chief of his own village, a man who'd been brought to know God through Matayo's living and practical Christianity.

Once again it was night. Once again the lamp hung from its nail. Ngoma was in bed watching what I was doing – to Matayo this time. As I ran blood into his veins the gardener pointed to his Bible.

'Bwana, God's book says, "The blood of Jesus Christ, God's Son, purifies us from all sin." *Yoh*, is it not the blood of the chief of my village that you are running into my arm? Is it not going to give me strength to beat the germs that came into my body through the mouth of the hyena? *Koh*, and is it not the blood of Jesus Christ, God's Son, that cleanses out the disease of sin and makes everlasting life mine?'

'Matayo, you've understood it clearly but behold, God's work is not like mine. I can repair people's ears, arms and legs but his work is no repair job. It makes us new people – new creatures.'

17
First Set

'Bwana,' said the tall Indian, 'I should like some of the white medicine for stomach pains.'

We were standing in our hospital dispensary. I nodded to Sila who was dressed in his best. He filled a bottle with the white mixture and handed it to the Indian.

'Well, Suliman, is there anything else we can do for you?'

'Yes, Bwana. I am bringing four of my relations on my return journey in the lorry. They have troublesome eyes and they need your medicine.'

'I'll be happy to see them. Now will you be good enough to take Sila to the railway. He is going on his first journey to the coast.'

'You've never seen the sea before, Sila?'

'No,' replied the African. 'I have never seen it.'

Suliman and I laughed.

Sila put his hand over his mouth and said, 'Don't laugh.'

But I couldn't help it. Both this young man's front teeth had been removed by me a month before and ever since he had lisped powerfully.

I gave Sila full instructions – whom to see, where to go and where to deliver several letters. A few minutes later we waved goodbye. After a tooting of horns and

much shouting the car went on its way and I turned back to my office. Pulling down a book I turned over a page marked, Sila. The first entry was in June, two years before.

I read: Pneumonia case. Carried in. Ten days in hospital. Given Sulphapyridine – cost ten shillings.

That had been our first contact with this Mugogo tribesman. He had been carried in by Christian relatives. He had fought a stiff battle with pneumonia but had reacted dramatically to the Sulpha drugs. I remembered how we had made him ward sweeper while still a convalescent and how hopelessly clumsy he had been at it. If there was anything upsettable, Sila would upset it.

When he was completely well he decided he would like to be a water carrier and so for some time he carried two kerosene tins full of water, suspended on a palm pole, across his shoulders. With three others he made fourteen trips a day to the wells ten kilometres away carrying 80 kilos' weight of water on each journey.

At first I wondered whether his health would stand it but good food and exercise built him up.

It was at this stage that I first met his grandfather – an old man with grizzled curly hair and two of the largest ear lobes I had ever seen. He came into hospital complaining of vague pains which he said, *jenda*, *jenda*, walked about haphazardly in his interior.

I made my diagnosis and called Sila aside.

'I'm afraid your grandfather will never get better. He has inside him what we call cancer but if he stays here we can save him pain and make his passing a kindlier one.'

The water carrier nodded. He had seen these cases before.

'Bwana, it would be a good thing to tell him. He is a man of courage. He does not fear death.'

'Why do you say this?' I asked.

'Well, Bwana, my grandfather was once a well known witchdoctor. He was called Mudeko. He removed evil spirits from people's stomachs and dislodged spells that had been cast against them.'

'How did he do all that?'

At this stage of his career Sila had two front teeth stuck out almost at right angles. To call them buckteeth would be a gross understatement. They looked like a dental verandah. When he grinned it could hardly be called a pretty sight but he did grin.

'Bwana,' he said, 'there are plants known to my grandfather which when cooked with goats' fat would make you very sick indeed. Now, if you thought you had a spell cast against you and you came to my grandfather, paid his fee which is a goat or a kerosene tin full of flour, he made his special medicine. You swallowed it and *yoh!* Were you sick! My grandfather had a special large clay bowl for this part of his treatment. When you had been sick he would put his hand into the bowl …'

'*Kumbe!* Stop it. That's a disgusting thing to do.'

Sila grinned again and I shuddered, partly because of the grin and partly because of his grandfather's horrid habits.

'What did he do then?'

'He would find inside the bowl bits of bone and hair – all sorts of things which, of course, he had put in there first. He would show these proudly as the cause and everybody would be happy.

'But all that, Bwana, was before he heard the words of God. He heard the words of the apostles speaking to the sorcerer. Now my grandfather had much money. All day long, was he not busy with his medicines? Did not people come from a long way away for his help? And then he heard the words from the Bible, "Your money perish with you because you thought that the gift of God could be purchased with money. Your heart is not right in the sight of God. Therefore repent."

'When he heard these words my grandfather was upset *kabisa!* He left his old ways and followed the ways of God.'

'Good. That's repentance – being sorry enough not to do it again.'

Sila nodded. 'Therefore, Bwana, seeing that he loves God and follows his way, why should he fear to die?'

'Quite,' I replied.

And so it came about that Sila came more and more into the ward. In the final illness of his grandfather he had been made the hospital hot water system. He carried out these onerous jobs by heating kerosene tins full of water over an open fire and carrying them to the places where they were wanted. He also became a primus expert.

Upon him had fallen the big job of sterilising all the instruments in the meningitis epidemic that hit us. What a hectic time that had been! Sick people poured in and I was unable to do the necessary minor operation to diagnose the disease because I was ill in bed. How I fussed and fretted as I lay there unable even to walk.

In had come Sila armed with a couple of test tubes. He smiled at me, 'Bwana, this is the spinal fluid from the two latest sick men.'

'What?' I exclaimed clinging onto the back of the bed and breathing as well as asthma would allow me. 'How did you collect that?'

Without blinking an eyelid Sila said, 'The usual way, Bwana, with the long needle. Have I not seen you do it a hundred times? Did I not follow the way that you did it? Is it not a simple work?'

And that was the beginning of his taking over quite a lot of the theatre work. Sila went on to become operating theatre assistant and later he learnt many of the ways to diagnose meningitis. He also learnt to use a stethoscope. Again and again he would go into the villages with my spare stethoscope round his neck and return with the news, 'I have found six people with the stabbing disease' which was his dramatic way of describing pneumonia. He would tell me, 'Have I not had this disease myself? Should I not recognise it in others?'

And then came the time when he became very sick, vaguely sick at first with pains here and there. His work was slipshod, his temper bad. For a long time I had warned him about his teeth. This old grandfather told me that when he was a small boy, in a drunken frenzy his father had bashed him in the mouth with a knobbed stick. The teeth had been loosened. When the broken jawbone had healed they had taken on this peculiar appearance. Now both those front teeth were dead. I pointed out to him that they were poisoning his system. He refused, however, to have anything done. He lay in hospital with his back towards anyone who tried to be sociable.

One day I came into the ward and heard a conversation. Yakobo, who was in charge of that ward, was talking. 'Sila, what good is it just to lie there? You make trouble for yourself and for everybody else that hears your complaining? It would be wiser to listen to the words of the Bwana.'

'No!' rapped out Sila. 'I won't. I refuse.'

'But listen,' said Yakobo, 'all your trouble will be over if you get rid of its cause. Has not the Bwana told you how sin is a poison, how it gets right through to our souls and weakens you and makes you wretched. In the end it kills your soul. Is not this poison from your teeth doing the same thing for your body?'

'*Kah!*' ground out Sila angrily. 'Go away. Go away. Go away!'

'But listen,' went on Yakobo quietly, 'you're not a good witness, a good advertisement for God. You say you believe in God and you behave like a bad-tempered small boy.'

Sila sat up furiously but the mere movement of sitting up caused him to groan. '*Yoh*,' he groaned, 'oh, my back!'

'*Hongo*,' said Yakobo, 'here is the Bwana. He will help you now.'

'Bwana,' said Sila. 'I have not eaten anything. Will you give me sleep medicine and take these teeth away? Anything to get rid of this pain.'

Before he could change his mind I boiled up instruments and an hour later the offending teeth were out.

'Ah,' said Yakobo looking at them, 'bad abscesses indeed.'

And now, a month later, Sila was up and about – quite his old, cheerful self again and on his way to the coast to be the first African from this tribe ever to have false teeth.

18
The Dog's Tail and the Tale's End

It was Friday afternoon. The junior dispenser had carefully washed out five kerosene tins. I went to the drawer, pulled out five prescriptions pasted onto cardboard and handed one to each of the dispensers.

Samson had a card with the prescription written normally and underneath it in the local language: White Medicine.

'*Kumbe*,' said Samson, 'this week I will bring comfort to many stomachs.'

Daudi's card read: Quinine mixture. He smiled and proceeded to weigh out that more than valuable drug in the treatment of malaria. This disease sweeps thousands into their graves in Africa.

'Don't lick your fingers, Daudi,' said Samson, 'or the medicine will bite you.'

The dispensers laughed and Daudi measured out a teaspoonful of a brilliant red dye and added it to his dispensing – his medicine was called: Red Mixture.

The two juniors were entrusted with a purple mixture which contained nothing more than bicarbonate of soda and peppermint. It was used exclusively for the inquisitive folk who turned up at hospital 'to taste the medicine of the Bwana.'

I myself was making the yellow mixture for the people who had dry coughs. We measured, mixed, stirred then poured litre after litre of medicine into huge stock bottles which were corked and placed on the table. There they sat, all the colours of the rainbow.

'Bwana,' said Daudi, 'it was a very good thought to colour all the medicines differently and then nobody makes a mistake.'

I nodded. 'Are all the tickets in order?'

He handed me a box. In it were large square tickets of all colours corresponding with the medicines. If you happened to be large and suffering from indigestion you received a large dose of white medicine. If you were middle-aged and suffering from malaria then it was a middle-sized dose of red quinine mixture. If you were small suffering from rheumatism then you were presented with a small black ticket and, of course, obtained a small dose of black medicine.

We put everything away and I checked the afternoon's activity.

Daudi came across to me.

'Bwana, I have three strangers who would like to see the work of our dispensary. They come from the country way over there.' He raised the pitch of his voice and pointed with his chin due north. 'They are members of our tribe and I met them when I was visiting my relations a week ago. They were travelling along the Great North Road near the signpost which reads: To Mvumi Hospital – 20 kms.'

'Bring them in and we'll show them what we do, and Kefa, go and tell the cook that I will drink tea with strangers. Make sure there's enough sugar.'

Kefa scampered off.

Looking round rather furtively our visitors came in. They were typical folk from the local tribe and as striking a cross section of the Wagogo as you could ask. The leader was an old man with tousled curly hair and a few struggling white bristles sprouting from his chin. His cheekbones were ornamented (it's all a matter of taste) with deep scars that radiated out beneath his eyes. His ears had been stretched so that they could reach halfway down to his shoulders and they contained a safety pin and a selection of bead ornaments. His chest was bare. He was dressed in a black cloth tied round his middle while his feet were protected from the roughness of the ground by cowhide sandals.

Beside him was a young warrior, mud in his hair and a pigtail half a metre long made from fibre and red mud. This trailed down his back. He had a cloth knotted over one shoulder and he strode along with the easy lope of one who finds a fifty kilometre walk in one day quite within his scope. He was armed with a two-metre-long spear – razor sharp.

The third of the trio was dressed in a dirty pair of shorts and armed with a knobbed stick.

I greeted them African fashion, going through the long rigmarole of greetings, and invited them to sit down on stools in the dispensary. They looked at all the medicines we had made that day.

'*Yah!*' said one, '*yali yehwanile mechila lya mbwa.*'

I translated this into English. '"This place where you make medicines is like the tail of a dog." That's a new one to me. I can't see any dog tails in this anywhere.'

Daudi threw back his head and laughed. 'Bwana, our people call the rainbow the tail of the dog.'

'*Hongo*, I see. But why the tail of the dog?'

'They call it that because when it comes the rain goes and also because out here many dogs' tails are curved.'

I turned to our visitors again. 'These are the medicines we make for sick people.'

'*Yoh*,' said the old man, 'my stomach bites these days.'

Kefa raised his eyebrows. I nodded. 'Give him some of the white medicine.'

The old man drank a glass noisily, ran his tongue round his lips and said, '*Yoh*, that's medicine.'

'It is indeed,' said Daudi. 'Do we not see many hundreds of people each week with stomachs that bite. This medicine will draw the teeth of any biting stomach.'

Then, of course, the other two wanted to taste it also. I had considerable difficulty in stopping them from having a sip from all the bottles that were in front of them.

'Bwana,' said Daudi, 'when I met these people over by the signpost that points to the hospital, they asked me where the road went. I told them and as we walked here I explained about the signpost of life, how Jesus talked to people and said, "I am the way and the truth and the life. No one comes to the father except through me. If you really knew me you would know my father as well. Anyone who had seen me has seen the father." *Eheeh*,' said Daudi, 'there are many ways to our hospital but there's only one way to God.'

The oldest man broke in. 'But, Bwana, we did not believe him. He told us of things that could not happen. Of men who had the disease of death (meningitis) and got better because of the medicine of the hospital. He told us of men who had been blind for years and who could see again after being treated at the hospital.'

The young warrior nodded his head. 'Truly, and he told us of ulcers as big as your hand that disappeared after injections.' He used the words: *when you stabbed people with the small needle.*

I smiled. 'And did he prove it?'

'*Heeeh*,' said the old man, 'my eyes were opened. We walked through the village and he said, "Come, and I will show you a man" and out came a young and strong man like my son here.' He pointed with his chin towards the young man with the pigtail.

'"Tell them about the disease of death".'

'"*Hongo*,' said the young man, 'my relations thought I was dead. My neck was stiff. My body was stiff. My head ached and my wisdom had departed. I remember lying in my house and then I found myself in a bed. Behold, my back was sore as though I had fallen on a thornbush. I was hungry and soon my wisdom returned and I was able to go back to my *kaya* all because they had the right medicine at the hospital".'

'Then we came to another village and I met an old man whom I knew. His name was Mesomabi, bad eyes. Had he not been blind for years? Did he not grope round the place until he came to the hospital and you worked on his eyes. Bwana, I knew that man was blind. He had tried every witchdoctor. It was only you who could help him.'

'*Koh*,' said Daudi. 'We met women whose children had all died till they were brought to our hospital. We saw men with healed ulcers – men whose teeth had been pulled out without pain. Now these three men are going to stay at Mvumi that they may learn the other side – the bigger side – of our work.'

The old man agreed.

'Indeed, these are words of truth,' I explained. 'We don't merely make better your sickness but we try to take from you the sting that's behind it all – the fear of death, the fear of evil.'

The man shivered.

'Daudi will tell you,' I went on, 'there is only one road to God. It's the way of a man who is also the Son of God. Jesus Christ is his name.'

At that moment the tea arrived and a noisy quarter-of-an-hour was enjoyed by all.

As I left them the old man said, 'May I come to the hospital each day, Bwana, to hear these words which speak of good news?'

'Certainly, Great One, that's what our hospital's for.'

THE JUNGLE DOCTOR SERIES

The Adventures Series
An ideal series to collect

Have you ever wanted to visit the rainforest? Have you ever longed to sail down the Amazon river? Would you just love to go on Safari in Africa? Well these books can help you imagine that you are actually there.

Pioneer missionaries retell their amazing adventures and encounters with animals and nature. In the Amazon you will discover tree frogs, piranha fish and electric eels. In the Rainforest you will be amazed at the armadillo and the toucan. In the blistering heat of the African Savannah you will come across lions and elephants and hyenas. And you will discover how God is at work in these amazing environments.

Rainforest Adventures by Horace Banner
ISBN 978-1-85792-627-9

African Adventures by Dick Anderson
ISBN 978-1-85792-807-5

Amazon Adventures by Horace Banner
ISBN 978-1-85792-440-4

Cambodian Adventures by Donna Vann
ISBN 978-1-84550-474-8

Great Barrier Reef Adventures by Jim Cromarty
ISBN 978-1-84550-068-9

Himalayan Adventures by Penny Reeve
ISBN 978-1-84550-080-1

Kiwi Adventures by Bartha Hill
ISBN 978-1-84550-282-9

New York City Adventures by Donna Vann
ISBN 978-1-84550-546-2

Outback Adventures by Jim Cromarty
ISBN 978-1-85792-974-4

Pacific Adventures by Jim Cromarty
ISBN 978-1-84550-475-5

Rainforest Adventures by Horace Banner
ISBN 978-1-85792-627-9

Rocky Mountain Adventures by Betty Swinford
ISBN 978-1-85792-962-1

Scottish Highland Adventures by Catherine Mackenzie
ISBN 978-1-84550-281-2

Wild West Adventures by Donna Vann
ISBN 978-1-84550-065-8

TRAILBLAZER SERIES

George Müller, The Children's Champion
ISBN 978-1-85792-549-4

Robert Murray McCheyne, Life is an Adventure
ISBN 978-1-85792-947-8

John Newton, A Slave Set Free
ISBN 978-1-85792-834-1

John Paton, A South Sea Island Rescue
ISBN 978-1-85792-852-5

Helen Roseveare, On His Majesty's Service
ISBN 978-1-84550-259-1

Mary Slessor, Servant to the Slave
ISBN 978-1-85792-348-3

Charles Spurgeon, Prince of Preachers
ISBN 978-1-84550-155-6

Patricia St. John, The Story Behind the Stories
ISBN 978-1-84550-328-4

Joni Eareckson Tada, Swimming against the Tide
ISBN 978-1-85792-833-4

Hudson Taylor, An Adventure Begins
ISBN 978-1-85792-423-7

John Welch, The Man who couldn't be Stopped
ISBN 978-1-85792-928-7

William Wilberforce, The Freedom Fighter
ISBN 978-1-85792-371-1

Richard Wurmbrand, A Voice in the Dark
ISBN 978-1- 85792-298-1

Start collecting this series now!

Ten Boys who used their Talents:
ISBN 978-1-84550-146-4

Paul Brand, Ghillean Prance, C.S.Lewis, C.T. Studd, Wilfred Grenfell, J.S. Bach, James Clerk Maxwell, Samuel Morse, George Washington Carver, John Bunyan.

Ten Girls who used their Talents:
ISBN 978-1-84550-147-1

Helen Roseveare, Maureen McKenna, Anne Lawson, Harriet Beecher Stowe, Sarah Edwards, Selina Countess of Huntingdon, Mildred Cable, Katie Ann MacKinnon, Patricia St. John, Mary Verghese.

Ten Boys who Changed the World:
ISBN 978-1-85792-579-1

David Livingstone, Billy Graham, Brother Andrew, John Newton, William Carey, George Müller, Nicky Cruz, Eric Liddell, Luis Palau, Adoniram Judson.

Ten Girls who Changed the World:
ISBN 978-1-85792-649-1

Corrie Ten Boom, Mary Slessor, Joni Eareckson Tada, Isobel Kuhn, Amy Carmichael, Elizabeth Fry, Evelyn Brand, Gladys Aylward, Catherine Booth, Jackie Pullinger.

Ten Boys who Made a Difference:
ISBN 978-1-85792-775-7

Augustine of Hippo, Jan Hus, Martin Luther, Ulrich Zwingli, William Tyndale, Hugh Latimer, John Calvin, John Knox, Lord Shaftesbury, Thomas Chalmers.

CHRISTIAN FOCUS PUBLICATIONS

Christian Focus | Christian Heritage | CF4K | Mentor

Christian Focus Publications publishes books for adults and children under its four main imprints: Christian Focus, CF4K, Mentor and Christian Heritage. Our books reflect that God's word is reliable and Jesus is the way to know him, and live for ever with him.

Our children's publication list includes a Sunday School curriculum that covers pre-school to early teens; puzzle and activity books. We also publish personal and family devotional titles, biographies and inspirational stories that children will love.

If you are looking for quality Bible teaching for children then we have an excellent range of Bible story and age specific theological books.

From pre-school to teenage fiction, we have it covered!

Find us at our web page:
www.christianfocus.com

CF4•K
Because you're never too young to know Jesus